Open[illegible]

Brian Tomlinson

Lingual House

First published 1986

Published by Lingual House
Beavor Lane
London W6 9AR

Typeset in Futura and Baskerville
by Katerprint Typesetting Services Ltd, Oxford
Printed and bound in Great Britain
By R J Acford, Chichester

British Library Cataloguing in Publication Data

Tomlinson, Brian
Openings.
1. English language——Text books for foreign speakers 2. Readers——Literature
I. Title
428.2'4

ISBN 0 86270 932 6

Contents

Acknowledgements

The author and publisher would like to thank the following for permission to reprint the extracts: Marion Boyars Publishers Ltd for Conflict 4; Jonathan Cape Ltd for Society 5 and Conflict 3; Marshall Cavendish International Ltd for Sport 2; Chatto & Windus Ltd for Conflict 2 and Family 5; William Collins Sons & Co. Ltd for Dilemmas 1; Constable & Co. Ltd for Growing Up 1; André Deutsch Ltd for Society 3; J.P. Donleavy for Family 6; East African Publishing House for Love 5; Faber and Faber Ltd for Sport 4 and Dilemmas 4; Granada Publishing Ltd for Sport 1; Graham Greene and The Bodley Head Ltd through Laurence Pollinger Ltd for Family 4 and Love 3; Hamish Hamilton Ltd for Society 2, © The Collection 1963 Hamish Hamilton, from *Vintage Thurber*; William Heinemann Ltd for Growing Up 2, Family 1 and Education 5; Heinemann Educational Books for Love 1 and Dilemmas 3; Michael Joseph Ltd for Family 2 and Sport 3; Methuen London for Society 9, from *Idandre and Other Poems*, and Conflict 1; Terry Morgan for Love 4; Shiva Naipaul and André Deutsch Ltd through Gillon Aitken for Education 2; Harold Ober Associates Inc. for Society 6, © 1968 by Copyright Administration Ltd; Penguin Books Ltd for Education 1, from *Yevtushenko: Selected Poems* © Robin Milner-Gulland and Peter Levi, 1962, and Society 1, from *Three Plays* by John Arden, © John Arden, 1961, 1962, 1964; A.D. Peters & Co. Ltd for Growing Up 4 and Society 8, and Growing Up 3 and Education 3; Martin Secker & Warburg Ltd for Education 4, Love 2 and Society 7; Sphere Books Ltd for Society 4; Keith Waterhouse and Michael Joseph Ltd through David Higham Associates Ltd for Family 3.

Illustrations and photographs are reproduced by permission of Liverpool Daily Post and Echo (p. 68); Michael Joseph Ltd (p. 113); BBC Hulton Picture Library (p. 121); Pablo Picasso, 'The Lovers', 1923, *DACS 1985*/National Gallery of Art, Washington, Chester Dale Collection (p. 127); Peter Clayton (p. 130); Age Concern England, Maria Bartha, and the Huddersfield Examiner (p. 133); Hamish Hamilton Ltd (p. 135); Paul Sample through Penny Field (p. 140); Pablo Picasso, 'Guernica', 1937, *DACS 1985* (p. 149).

Introduction

Openings is a collection of extracts from 'literature' in English. The extracts are taken from books written all over the world and the focus is on English as an international language.

The book is intended for learners of English as a second or foreign language in any country in the world and is designed to help them to improve their English in a stimulating, creative and educationally useful way.

The extracts have been chosen for their value in giving learners an enjoyment in reading, an interesting and rich exposure to English in use, and a broadening experience of the world. They have been selected mainly from contemporary literature and will provide readers with relevant content and variety of expression. The extracts are presented in thematic units so that they can be combined and compared; within each unit they are arranged in approximate order of difficulty, ranging from lower intermediate to advanced.

The emphasis in the book is on creative reading rather than study and the texts are intended to stimulate communicative activities rather than to exemplify genres of English literature. They can thus be used by all types of EFL learners, from pupils in secondary schools to students in language schools and from learners of English for specific purposes to advanced students of English literature. The ideal aim is to open up Literature in English, to show that it can be accessible and rewarding and thus to encourage learners to read extensively on their own. The second, probably more realistic, aim for many learners is to use literature to open up possibilities for using English in intelligent, creative ways. This can help the learners not only to develop their abilities in English, but to develop as human beings as well.

The objective of the book is enrichment; the main means of achieving it can only be enjoyment.

The value of literature in TEFL

For many learners of EFL English Literature is associated with laborious tedium. Their experience consists mainly of answering difficult questions on difficult texts and of being forced to read books of no apparent relevance to their own lives.

The result is no enjoyment and very little gain. However, it has been my experience in Europe, in Africa and in the South Pacific that it is possible for the majority of any group of EFL learners to gain enjoyment and considerable profit from reading literature, providing that the teacher helps to make the texts accessible and relevant and that the learners are given some say in what they read and how they read it.

When such positive conditions have been created the following benefits have resulted.

1 *Enrichment of intake*

Intake is the language 'selected' by the brain for processing from all the language the learner is exposed to. Significance, impact, stimulus and enjoyment seem to be important criteria for 'selection'. Literature can satisfy these criteria and thus provide an intake which is rich in potential information about authentic use of language (i.e. about the interaction between content, context, purpose and style).

2 *Focus on content*

All literature, by definition, has content. It conveys information, ideas, attitudes and views. It appeals to the whole person rather than just the language learner, and it can therefore facilitate informal language acquisition through motivated exposure and use.

3 *Real use of reading skills*

Responding to literature involves using such skills as prediction, deduction of meaning, inferring attitude, skimming, scanning and detecting and interpreting presuppositions. It thus provides the opportunity to use the reading skills taught during the course and it contributes to the development of those skills.

4 *Stimulus for other language activities*

Because literature can make an impact and be provocative and stimulating, it can be a useful starting point for activities which involve analysis and discussion and it can also inspire creativity in the learners' responses.

5 *Motivation*

Providing the learners have some say in the choice of texts and are not forced to 'study', then literature can motivate even the most reluctant learners because of its appeal to their humanity.

6 *Experience*
Reading literature in English can provide the learners with experience of cultures and people otherwise inaccessible to them, and it can thus serve the crucial educational function of broadening the mind.

7 *Self-access*
Learners who gain enjoyment from reading literature in English at school are given a means of continuing to acquire English outside the classroom and after leaving school.

In short, literature can open up and enrich the language class. It can also provide motivated, purposeful, active exposure to authentic language in ways which involve using (rather than practising) language and responding as an individual human being rather than as a member of a group of language learners.

What is in *Openings*?

Part I

Part I consists of forty-two texts taken from modern literature in English.
The texts are presented without introductions, glossaries or activities. This is so that the teacher and learners can use them in any way they want, and so that when the texts are being read the learners can respond to them without impediment and without worrying about any extra-textual demands.

Part II

Part II consists of activities which can be used with the texts from Part I. Each text in Part I has accompanying pre-, whilst- and post-reading activities, but obviously teachers are free to devise supplementary or replacement activities of their own.

Bibliography

An index of the books which the extracts in *Openings* are taken from.

List of Authors

An index of the authors who are used in *Openings* plus brief sketches of the authors and suggestions for further reading which might appeal to learners at this level.

Ways of Using this Book

Suggested approaches

1 Let different individuals or groups work out a reading programme for the term after skimming through the book and sampling some of the texts. The programme could be based on one or more than one thematic unit or could consist of a list of individual texts selected for their apparent appeal.

Learners who have read the same text should be encouraged to discuss their reactions to it and to take part in the follow-up activities together.

N.B.:

a) The initial reading programme should be considered provisional and able to be altered at any time after consultation with the teacher.

b) The learners should be encouraged (but not forced) to read some of the books the extracts are taken from and to find and read other texts relevant to those they have read in the book.

2 All the learners skim the book and sample some of the texts, and then each learner writes down five texts he or she wants to read. The teacher analyses the choices and selects a number of 'popular' texts to focus on for the term.

N.B.:

a) In each 'literature' lesson the teacher can ask all the learners to read and respond to the same text or can offer each learner two or more alternative texts to select from.

b) After most of the selected texts have been read the teacher can present the learners with a 'library' of the books which the extracts have been taken from and can invite each learner to choose and read one or more of the books.

3 As for 2, but the learners are asked to select one or more of the themes. The teacher analyses the choices and decides which of the most popular ones to choose for the term. The learners and the teacher then decide which of the texts to read.

After the texts have been read and responded to, the learners can be asked to find other materials relevant to the theme.

N.B.:

a) Different individuals or groups can read different texts and then get together to share what they have read.
b) The reading can be part of the preparatory stage before a written or oral presentation of a paper by an individual or group or part of a creative writing project relevant to the theme.

4 The learners are given the book and then told that they have a particular period of time (e.g. half a term) to sample the texts with a view to deciding on a number of books (e.g. five) they want to be included in their class library and on a number of books (e.g. two) which they want to read as class texts.

During the sampling period the learners are given time in class and for homework to read texts from the book, and are encouraged to talk to each other and to the teacher about what they have read.

At the end of the sampling period decisions are made by the class and the teacher about which books to put in the class library and which to read together as class texts. Obviously such practical considerations as how much money is available and which books are already in stock in the school will influence the final decisions.

5 The teacher selects themes and texts for the term suitable for the levels, interests and backgrounds of the learners.

Types of activities used

A Pre-reading activities

Pre-reading activities are designed to be done before the learners read the texts so as to focus their attention and interest on the theme or topic of the text, to help make the text more accessible, to motivate the learners to want to read the text and to give them a purpose for reading it. The following are some examples.

1 Predicting the content of a text from a title or illustration or other clues, e.g.

a) predicting from the title and stage directions of *The Birthday Party* (Conflict 1);
b) predicting 'Schoolmaster' (Education 1) from a drawing of a sad man looking out of a window.

2 Predicting the content of a text from one or more of its paragraphs, e.g. paragraph 9 of *A Dream of Africa* (Dilemmas 1).
N.B.: The paragraph(s) can be photocopied, typed out, written on the board, dictated or read aloud.

3 Group discussion of a topic relevant to the theme of a text, e.g.
   a) discussion of the misunderstandings between teenagers and their parents before reading *The Graduate* (Growing Up 1);
   b) discussion of the obligations of grown-up children to their ageing parents before reading *The Right True End* (Family 2).

4 Listening to a short story or anecdote relevant to the content of the text, e.g.
   a) the teacher tells a story about his or her first day as a teacher before the class reads *The Natural Order* (Education 4);
   b) learners tell each other the plots of any spy films they have seen before they read *Twinkle, Twinkle Little Spy* (Conflict 3).

5 The learners are asked to find and tell short stories about a particular theme, e.g.
   a) stories about a first date before reading *Looks and Smiles* (Sport 3);
   b) stories about bureaucracy before reading *The British Museum is Falling Down* (Dilemmas 2).

6 Groups of learners are asked to share all they know about a topic before reading a relevant text, e.g.
   a) Vietnam before reading 'On the Yankee Station' (Conflict 5);
   b) Muhammad Ali before reading *The Greatest* (Sport 1);
   c) the treatment of the insane before reading *One Flew Over the Cuckoo's Nest* (Conflict 4);
   d) the Women's Liberation Movement before reading the second extract from *The World According to Garp* (Society 8).

7 Groups of learners are encouraged to share their own personal experiences of the subject of a text before reading it, e.g.
   a) recalling a teacher they had strong feelings about before reading *Unreliable Memoirs* (Growing Up 3);
   b) talking about things that frightened them when they were very young before they read the first extract from *The World According to Garp* (Growing Up 4).

8 Recalling the main points of one extract so that they can compare it with a new text as they read it, e.g.
noting down the main points of *The Happy Haven* (Society 1) before reading *The Right True End* (Family 2).

N.B.: Each text in Part I of *Openings* has accompanying pre-reading activities in Part II. However, the teacher might like to add to them or replace them by using the ideas above.

B Whilst-reading activities

These are activities done whilst the learners are reading the text in order to make it more accessible to them and to engage them in purposeful interaction with the text. The following are some examples.

1 Listening to a good reading (by the teacher or on tape) of a lively extract from the text. The extract should ideally be fairly short and have potential for grabbing and retaining the attention and interest of the listeners. Lively dialogues, descriptions of exciting events and poetry and prose which evoke mood or atmosphere are examples of the types of extracts which can make a text more meaningful and appealing if read aloud well. Such extracts can be found, for example, in:

a) 'Telephone Conversation' (Society 9);
b) *Midnight's Children* (Society 5);
c) *The British Museum is Falling Down* (Dilemmas 2);
d) *A Man For All Seasons* (Dilemmas 3);
e) *The Graduate* (Growing Up 1);
f) 'Schoolmaster' (Education 1).

2 Checking against predictions previously made about the text, e.g.
a) checking predictions made about 'Sentence of Death' (Love 4) from the title and the illustration;
b) checking predictions made about 'Schoolmaster' (Education 1) from the drawing of the man looking out of a window.

3 Drawing one of the characters or a scene from the story whilst reading, e.g.
a) drawing the 'stoning' of Beverley Hindmarsh from *Unreliable Memoirs* (Growing Up 3);
b) drawing the examination of Naseem from *Midnight's Children* (Society 5).

4 Completing charts, profiles, flow charts etc. whilst reading the text, e.g.
a) completing a flow chart of events in *Close Encounters of the Third Kind* (Society 4);
b) completing profiles of specified characters in *The Heart of the Matter* (Love 3).

5 Mentally answering questions that were copied from the board before reading the text, e.g.
   a) questions on the main targets of satire in *Indecent Exposure* (Society 7);
   b) questions on Mann's objectives and strategies in *Twinkle, Twinkle Little Spy* (Conflict 3).

6 Talking aloud to the author or one of the characters whilst reading the text, e.g.
   a) talking to the Big Nurse in *One Flew Over the Cuckoo's Nest* (Conflict 4);
   b) talking to Benjamin in *The Graduate* (Growing Up 1).

7 Visualization of the scene described in the text with a view to describing it to someone who has not read the text, and then answering questions about it, e.g.
   a) *The Heart of the Matter* (Love 3);
   b) *The Interpreters* (Society 3).

8 Discussion about problems in the text whilst pairs of learners read a shared text, e.g.
   a) *One Flew Over the Cuckoo's Nest* (Conflict 4);
   b) *Forty Years On* (Dilemmas 4).

N.B.:

1 Most of the texts in Part I have accompanying whilst-reading activities in Part II. However, the teacher could use one of the ideas above to add to or replace the activities suggested for a particular text in Part II.

2 One of the most useful whilst-reading activities is to get two or more learners to read a text together for a particular purpose and to talk to each other about the text as they read it.

3 The teacher should be careful only to set whilst-reading activities which help the reader and not to set activities which are so demanding that they put the learners off reading the text.

C Post-reading activities

These are activities done after reading the text in order to check recall, check understanding, stimulate thought and discussion, provide opportunities for interaction, or stimulate 'creative' use of language. The following are some examples.

Recall

1 Group miming of the events in the extract, e.g.
   a) *The British Museum is Falling Down* (Dilemmas 2);
   b) *Midnight's Children* (Society 5);
   c) *The Interpreters* (Society 3).

2 Individuals or groups telling the story to those who have not read it. This can be done by different individuals or groups reading different extracts and then pairing up and swapping stories, e.g.
   a) *The Chip-Chip Gatherers* (Education 2) and *Unreliable Memoirs* (Education 3);
   b) *Twinkle, Twinkle Little Spy* (Conflict 3) and *The Human Factor* (Family 4).

3 A group of learners who have read the same text sit in a circle and retell the story as a chain story (i.e. they take it in turns to tell parts of the story), e.g.
   a) *The World According to Garp* (Society 8);
   b) *The Natural Order* (Education 4).

4 Groups of learners who have read the same text select the true statements from a number of statements about what happens in the text and then order them in the same sequence as in the text, e.g.
   a) statements about what Big Nurse does in *One Flew Over the Cuckoo's Nest* (Conflict 4);
   b) statements about what happens in *How Far Can You Go?* (Love 2).

5 Visual representation of the story in the text, e.g.
   a) a picture strip cartoon of *A Dream of Africa* (Dilemmas 1);
   b) a group painting of the examination of Naseem in *Midnight's Children* (Society 5).

Understanding

1 Working out from clues in the extract information about the setting, characters and plot of the novel it is taken from, e.g.
   a) *The Heart of the Matter* (Love 3);
   b) *The Human Factor* (Family 4).

2 Working out from clues in the extract what happens in the book immediately before and after the extract, e.g.
   a) *The World According to Garp* (Society 8);
   b) 'On the Yankee Station' (Conflict 5).

3 Pair/group dramatization of a text the learners have read, e.g.
   a) *The Graduate* (Growing Up 1);
   b) *The Interpreters* (Society 3);
   c) *The Ginger Man* (Family 6).

4 Debates on themes from the extracts, e.g.
   a) 'The State Should Provide Accommodation and Care for the Old': *The Right True End* (Family 2) and *The Happy Haven* (Society 1);
   b) 'Religions Should Not Be Allowed to Determine What People Should Think and Do': *Midnight's Children* (Society 5) and *A Man For All Seasons* (Dilemmas 3).

5 Balloon debates in which learners play characters from the texts which have been read and try to justify being kept in the basket whilst someone else is thrown out to reduce the weight and stop the balloon from dropping to the ground, e.g. the teacher from 'Schoolmaster' (Education 1), Pfitz from 'On the Yankee Station' (Conflict 5) and Chamberlain from *Forty Years On* (Dilemmas 4).

6 In groups, learners interview the author (played by one of the group) about why he wrote the book, play, poem or story and what he was trying to say in it, e.g.
   a) *One Flew Over the Cuckoo's Nest* (Conflict 4);
   b) 'Sentence of Death' (Love 4);
   c) 'My Name Blew Like a Horn Among the Payira' (Love 5).

7 In groups, learners play policemen, researchers, investigators, journalists etc. and 'interview' a character (or characters) from a text, e.g.
   a) the characters in *The Heart of the Matter* (Love 3) are questioned by a private investigator about what happened during the night;
   b) the characters in *Professional Foul* (Sport 4) are interrogated by the police.

8 Characters from the texts (played by learners) are put on trial to defend their actions, e.g.
   a) Pfitz is accused of victimizing Lydecker in 'On the Yankee Station' (Conflict 5);
   b) Mann is accused of cruelty towards Bekuv in *Twinkle, Twinkle Little Spy* (Conflict 3).

9 Group discussion of controversial statements, e.g.
   a) 'Thomas More was a Selfish Man' in *A Man For All Seasons* (Dilemmas 3).
   b) 'Garp had no Right to go to the Women's Meeting and Deserved What Happened to Him' in *The World According to Garp* (Society 8).

Creative activities

1 Designing a front cover for the book, e.g.
   a) *Journey to Wembley* (Sport 2);
   b) *A Dream of Africa* (Dilemmas 1);
   c) *One Flew Over the Cuckoo's Nest* (Conflict 4).

2 Painting a personal interpretation of the text, e.g.
   a) *The World According to Garp* (Growing Up 4);
   b) *Close Encounters of the Third Kind* (Society 4);
   c) 'My Name Blew Like a Horn Among the Payira' (Love 5).

3 Writing the next verse, scene, chapter etc., e.g.
   a) the next chapter of *The Heart of the Matter* (Love 3);
   b) the next scene of *The Birthday Party* (Conflict 1).

4 Rewriting the text from a different viewpoint, e.g.
   a) rewriting 'Schoolmaster' (Education 1) so that it is written by the teacher;
   b) rewriting the 'stoning' scene from *Unreliable Memoirs* (Growing Up 3) so that it is written by Darryl.

5 Rewriting the text to include a change in the events, e.g.
   a) rewriting *The Graduate* (Growing Up 1) so that Ben's father is trying to persuade him to come down to see his fiancée;
   b) rewriting the end of the extract from *The Heart of the Matter* (Love 3) so that 'he' returns home to find Louise waiting for him in bed.

6 Rewriting the text in a different style, e.g. rewriting part of *One Flew Over the Cuckoo's Nest* (Conflict 4) so that it is written in a simple, straightforward narrative style without detailed descriptions.

7 Rewriting the text to include an additional character, e.g.
   a) adding McCann's friend to *The Birthday Party* (Conflict 1);
   b) adding Mrs Braddock to *The Graduate* (Growing Up 1).

8 Changing the medium, e.g.
   a) changing 'Schoolmaster' (Education 1) into a short story;
   b) changing *The Natural Order* (Education 4) into a scene from a play;
   c) changing *The Birthday Party* (Conflict 1) into the beginning of a novel.

9 Writing a version of the text in the first language after reading it carefully and then giving it back to the teacher.

10 Changing the text into a picture strip cartoon and adding to the story, e.g.
   a) *How Far Can You Go?* (Love 2);
   b) 'Sentence of Death' (Love 4).

11 Writing a film script for a scene from a book, e.g.
   a) *The Heart of the Matter* (Love 3);
   b) *How Far Can You Go?* (Love 2);
   c) *The Interpreters* (Society 3).

12 Composing a song based on the text, e.g.
   a) 'Schoolmaster' (Education 1);
   b) *The World According to Garp* (Growing Up 4).

13 Turning a text into dance drama, e.g.
   a) *The Heart of the Matter* (Love 3);
   b) *The Greatest – My Own Story* (Sport 1);
   c) 'My Name Blew Like a Horn Among the Payira' (Love 5).

14 Writing original stories, poems etc. based on the same theme(s), e.g.
   a) a story about going overseas alone for the first time, based on *A Dream of Africa* (Dilemmas 1);
   b) a story about someone making great sacrifices, based on the theme from *A Man For All Seasons* (Dilemmas 3).

N.B.:

1 Most of the above activities are best done in pairs or groups, so that the learners can help and learn from each other. The oral interaction between the learners adds a valuable dimension to the activity.

2 The above activities do not work successfully if imposed on reluctant learners. It is therefore important that the learners are given a say in what activities they do (either by letting the class or group decide from a number of options or by setting up a number of activities and then letting individuals decide which one(s) they want to do.

3 After experiencing some of the possible follow-up activities learners can become quite good at working out their own follow-up activities, and this independence should certainly be encouraged.

4 It is important the teacher and the learners view these activities as learning experiences and not as tests. In order to achieve this the teacher needs to act as stimulator, facilitator, guide and participant rather than as assessor and corrector.

5 The success of these activities should be judged as much on the motivation and participation of the learners as on the quality of the end product.

6 Each text in Part I has accompanying post-reading exercises in Part II. However, the teacher might like to add to them or replace them by using some of the ideas above.

Examples of lesson plans using texts from the book

The Under Toad

1 The teacher tells the class about something he was very frightened of when he was very young.

2 The learners tell each other about their childhood fears and discuss how they arose and how they were overcome.

3 The teacher tells the class to imagine they are small children who have been told that they should not swim in the sea because of the dangerous Under Toad. In groups the learners try to picture (and possibly draw) what the Under Toad looks like.

4 The learners are given the extract from *The World According to Garp* by John Irving (Growing Up 4) and are told to read it to find out what the Under Toad meant to Walt when he was a small boy and what it came to mean to the family later.

5 The learners (in groups) are told to refer to the text to work out answers to the following questions:
a) What is the relationship between:
Garp and Helen?
Garp and Walt?
Walt and Duncan?
b) Where do you think Garp and Duncan are going?
c) Why do you think Helen and Walt are not with them?
d) What do you think the last paragraph means?

6 In groups the learners either:
a) write a short poem about the Under Toad as though it was written by Walt

OR

b) write the next two paragraphs of the novel.

7 The groups look at each other's work and make suggestions for improvement.

Schoolmaster

1 a) The learners are told to close their eyes and visualize a teacher they remember from primary school. They then tell each other about their teachers and what they can remember about them.

OR

b) The learners (in groups) are given a photograph or drawing of a sad man looking out of a window and are asked to work out who and where he is and what he is doing.

2 a) The teacher tells the class he or she is going to read a poem aloud and that during the reading the learners should close their eyes and visualize exactly what is happening in the poem. He tells them the poem is written by a pupil about his teacher.

OR

b) The teacher tells the learners that he or she is going to read a poem about the man in the picture and that during the reading they should check their predictions about the man and what he is doing.

3 The teacher reads aloud 'Schoolmaster' (Education 1).

4 The teacher gets the class to say what information the poem tells us about the Schoolmaster.

5 The teacher refers the learners to the poem and tells them to read it and whilst they are doing so to consider the following questions:
a) What is different about the attention of the class?
b) Why do you think the Schoolmaster's wife has left him?
c) Why do the pupils watch in silence?
d) Where do you think he is going when he walks out into the snow?

6 The learners decide which one of the following activities to do and then work either individually or with others who have chosen the same activity.
a) Write a short poem about one of your primary school teachers.
b) Rewrite 'Schoolmaster' so that it becomes the beginning of a novel narrated by the teacher.
c) Write a scene from a play in which the Schoolmaster finds his wife.
d) Write a version of the poem in your first language.
e) Write an extract from a film script giving directions for the filming of the scene described in the poem.

Bureaucracy

1 For homework the learners are asked to find jokes or satirical stories about bureaucracy.

2 The learners form groups and tell each other their jokes etc.

3 Each group chooses one joke or story and tells it to the rest of the class.

4 The teacher talks with the class about reference libraries, about the staff and uses of such libraries and about the British Museum Reading Room.

5 The learners read the extract from *The British Museum is Falling Down* by David Lodge (Dilemmas 2) and as they read they imagine how they would turn it into a scene from a play.

6 The learners form groups of four (A, first man, second man, and a director) and then work out and rehearse their version of the scene from the play.

7 Pairs of groups are formed and each group performs its scene for the other member of its pair.

8 For homework each learner writes a short sketch satirizing aspects of bureaucracy.

9 Each learner shows his sketch to the other members of his group.

10 Each group selects one of their members' sketches and rehearses it.

11 Each group performs its sketch for the rest of the class.

N.B.:

1 Each of the texts in Part I has accompanying activities in Part II which can be put together to form a lesson plan. However, the teacher (or the learners) might like to make their own lesson plan for using a text based on some of the suggested activities in Part II and/or some of the ideas above.

2 The activities in Part II are designed for use with specific texts. There are no activities which invite comparison of texts or linking with other texts as it is not the intention to impose texts on learners. However, it is

obviously a good idea if learners are asked to compare texts in the book which they have read and to relate them to other thematically similar texts they have read.

3 Creative writing tasks based on the texts in Part I are often most valuable if they are done by small groups working together to write one text. This encourages them to pool their experiences, ideas and vocabularies, to stimulate each other to produce ideas, to learn from each other and to develop both oral and written communication skills as they work.

List of Extracts

5 Society

6 Sport

7 Conflict

8 Dilemmas

Part I

Extracts from Modern Literature

Growing Up

1 The Graduate

Charles Webb

Part One

1

Benjamin Braddock graduated from a small Eastern college on a day in June. Then he flew home. The following evening a party was given for him by his parents. By eight o'clock most of the guests had arrived but Benjamin had not yet come down from his room. His father called up from the foot of the stairs but there was no answer. Finally he hurried up the stairs and to the end of the hall.

'Ben?' he said, opening his son's door.

'I'll be down later,' Benjamin said.

'Ben, the guests are all here,' his father said. 'They're all waiting.'

'I said I'll be down later.'

Mr Braddock closed the door behind him. 'What is it,' he said.

Benjamin shook his head and walked to the window.

'What is it, Ben.'

'Nothing.'

'Then why don't you come on down and see your guests.'

Benjamin didn't answer.

'Ben?'

'Dad,' he said, turning around, 'I have some things on my mind right now.'

'What things.'

'Just some things.'

'Well can't you tell me what they are?'

'No.'

Mr Braddock continued frowning at his son a few more moments, glanced at his watch, then looked back at Benjamin. 'Ben, these are our friends down there,' he said. 'My friends. Your mother's friends. You owe them a little courtesy.'

'Tell them I have to be alone right now.'

'Mr Robinson's out in the garage looking at your new sports car. Now go on down and give him a ride in it.'

Benjamin reached into his pocket for a pair of shiny keys on a small chain. 'Here,' he said.

'What?'

'Give him the keys. Let him drive it.'

'But he wants to see you.'

'Dad, I don't want to see him right now,' Benjamin said. 'I don't want to see the Robinsons, I don't want to see the Pearsons, I don't want to see the . . . the Terhunes.'

'Ben, Mr Robinson and I have been practicing law together in this town for seventeen years. He's the best friend I have.'

'I realize that.'

'He has a client over in Los Angeles that he's put off seeing so he could be here and welcome you home from college.'

'Dad –'

'Do you appreciate that?'

'I'd appreciate it if I could be alone!'

His father shook his head. 'I don't know what's got into you,' he said, 'but whatever it is I want you to snap out of it and march right on down there.'

Suddenly the door opened and Benjamin's mother stepped into the room. 'Aren't you ready yet?' she said.

'No.'

'We'll be right down,' his father said.

'Well what's wrong,' she said, closing the door behind her.

'I am trying to think!'

'Come on, Ben,' his father said. He took his arm and began leading him toward the door.

'Goddammit will you leave me alone!' Benjamin said. He pulled away and stood staring at him.

'Ben?' Mr Braddock said quietly, staring back at him, 'don't you ever swear at your mother or me again.'

Benjamin shook his head. Then he walked between them and to the door. 'I'm going for a walk,' he said. He stepped out into the hall and closed the door behind him.

2 No Longer at Ease

Chinua Achebe

CHAPTER SEVEN

Obi's first day in the Civil Service was memorable, almost as memorable as his first day at the bush mission school in Umuofia nearly twenty years before. In those days white men were very rare. In fact, Mr Jones had been the second white man Obi had set eyes on, and he had been nearly seven then. The first white man had been the Bishop of the Niger.

Mr Jones was the Inspector of Schools and was feared throughout the province. It was said that he had fought during the Kaiser's war and that it had gone to his head. He was a huge man, over six feet tall. He rode a motor-cycle which he always left about half a mile away so that he could enter a school unannounced. Then he was sure to catch somebody committing an offence. He visited a school about once in two years and he always did something which was remembered until his next visit. Two years before, he had thrown a boy out of a window. Now it was the headmaster who got into trouble. Obi never discovered what the trouble was because it had all been done in English. Mr Jones was red with fury as he paced up and down, taking such ample strides that at one point Obi thought he was making straight for him. The headmaster, Mr Nduka, was all the while trying to explain something.

'Shut up!' roared Mr Jones, and followed it up with a slap. Simeon Nduka was one of those people who had taken to the ways of the white man rather late in life. And one of the things he had learnt in his youth was the great art of wrestling. In the twinkling of an eye Mr Jones was flat on the floor and the school was thrown into confusion. Without knowing why, teachers and pupils all took to their heels. To throw a white man was like unmasking an ancestral spirit.

That was twenty years ago. Today few white men would dream of slapping a headmaster in his school and none at all would actually do it. Which is the tragedy of men like William Green, Obi's boss.

Obi had already met Mr Green that morning. As soon as he had arrived he had been taken in to be introduced to him. Without rising from his seat or offering his hand Mr Green muttered something to the effect that Obi would enjoy his work; one, if he wasn't bone-lazy, and two, if he was prepared to use his loaf. 'I'm assuming you have one to use,' he concluded.

A few hours later he appeared in Mr Omo's office where Obi had been posted for the day. Mr Omo was the Administrative Assistant. He had put nearly thirty years' service into thousands of files, and would retire, or so he said, when his son had completed his legal studies in England. Obi was spending his first day in Mr Omo's office to learn a few things about office administration.

Mr Omo jumped to his feet as soon as Mr Green came in. Simultaneously he pocketed the other half of the kola nut he was eating.

'Why hasn't the Study Leave file been passed to me?' Mr Green asked.

'I thought . . .'

'You are not paid to think, Mr Omo, but to do what you are told. Is that clear? Now send the file to me immediately.'

'Yes, sir.'

Mr Green slammed the door behind him and Mr Omo carried the file personally to him. When he returned he began to rebuke a junior clerk who, it seemed, had caused all the trouble.

Obi had now firmly decided that he did not like Mr Green and that Mr Omo was one of his old Africans. As if to confirm his opinion the telephone rang. Mr Omo hesitated as he always did when the telephone rang, and then took it up as if it was liable to bite.

'Hello. Yes, sir.' He handed it over to Obi with obvious relief. 'Mr Okonkwo, for you.'

Obi took the telephone. Mr Green wanted to know whether he had received a formal offer of appointment. Obi said, no, he hadn't.

'You say *sir* to your superior officers, Mr Okonkwo,' and the telephone was dropped with a deafening bang.

3 Unreliable Memoirs

Clive James

Admittedly some of the local adults were terrifying. Gail Thorpe's husband Wally was a pastry cook whose business had failed. His principal means of revenge was to brow-beat his wife, who went away for electric convulsion therapy every year or so. The only result of the treatment was to alter the position of her nervous smile, so that instead of being on the front of her face it ended up under one ear. By the time it drifted around to the front again she was ready for another course of treatment. Wally also tormented his children in various ways. He would go on tickling his younger daughter, Carmel, long after the desperately sobbing child had begged him to stop. Watching these performances, I woke up early to the reality of human evil. News of mass political atrocity has always saddened me but never come as a surprise. The only time I tried to interfere with one of Wally Thorpe's divertissements, he swore at me for ten minutes on end at the top of his voice. I went home stunned. My mother did her best to tell him off but it was clear that at such moments she sorely felt her loneliness. That night was one of the few times I ever heard her say, 'I wish your father had come home.'

The Goodhews were likewise a bit of a pain. They were so protective about their sons, Darryl and Des, that they would trail them about, checking up on what was going on. This could be awkward when what was going on was a full-scale battle involving the throwing of stones and bits of fibro. These battles usually took place up in the quarry, with the defenders occupying fox-holes in the heights and the attackers moving up through the lowlands from one clump of lantana to another. Very properly concerned about their children losing an eye, the Goodhew parents would invariably show up just in time to see one of their little darlings sconed by a rock or sliced open by a whizzing piece of fibro. The fuss would take weeks to die down. According to Mr and Mrs Goodhew, their children were being led astray by the local toughs. In fact their own progeny were the worst of the lot. Darryl Goodhew could look wonderfully innocent when his parents were around, but he was a dead shot when they weren't looking. He once knocked Beverley Hindmarsh off her dinkey at an incredible range. The missile was a lump of sandstone. He was sharing a fox-hole with me at the top of the quarry. It was the best fox-hole: you had to crawl through a lantana tunnel to get to it. Halfway down Margaret Street, Beverley was a dot on the horizon when Darryl launched his rock. It was a long time on its way. I had lost sight of it long before she abruptly stopped pedalling and crashed sideways with awful finality. Darryl immediately ran towards the scene of the crime with a look of concern. His air of innocence was so persuasive that Beverley's parents never thought of blaming him. They would have blamed me if I had been stupid enough to emerge from the lantanas. I was already established as Beverley's persecutor, having pinched her bottom one day with a metal reinforcing clip stolen from a building site. It was meant to be a joke, but it took a piece out of her pointed behind. I got belted for that, and if I surfaced now I would get belted again. Besides, Darryl would undoubtedly have pointed the finger at me. So I stayed up there until the stars came out. Beverley suffered nothing more severe than shock and a badly bruised infantile bud. When you consider that the stone might just as easily have removed an eyeball, you can see that we must have had a guardian angel.

Otherwise the adults left us pretty much alone. On the week ends we made our big expeditions to the pictures, the swamp or the dump. In the afternoons and evenings after school we played in the street. We played cock-a-lorum from one side of the street to the other. We played a game with half a dozen sticks spaced out along the front strip and you were allowed to take only one step between every two sticks. You kept moving the sticks further and further apart until nobody was left in except some visiting kid built like a praying mantis. You had to do as many chin-ups as you could on the box tree. There were complicated bike races around the block. The older boys did a lot of elaborate riding up and down in front of the girls, who used to sit in line on the Chappelows' front fence. Warren Hartigan could sit on his bicycle backwards and ride past very slowly. They stopped giggling when he did that. Graham Truscott should never have tried it. A spoke from one of the wheels went right through his calf.

We played hidings and countries. In countries you threw a tennis ball in the air and ran, calling out the name of a country. Each player had the name of a country. If your country was called, you tried to catch the ball before it bounced, whereupon you could throw it up again and call out somebody else's country. If you only caught it on the bounce, you had to . . . Forget it. The rules went on and on. All that mattered was to throw the ball high. Greg Brennan could put it into orbit. He lived next door but one. Nobody lived very far away. We played on and on through the hot afternoon into the brief dusk and the sudden nightfall. Towards sunset the adults would appear on the front porches and start watering the lawn. They would tune the nozzles to a fine spray, which would drift in the air at the first breath of the summer wind that came every night. Usually it was a nor'easter. Sometimes it was the Southerly Buster. The Christmas beetles and cowboy beetles held jamborees around the street-lights, battering themselves against the white enamel reflectors and falling into the street. They lay on their backs with their legs struggling. When you picked them up they pulsed with the frustrated strength of their clenched wing muscles.

Before there was the refrigerator there was the ice-chest. A block of ice was loaded into it every couple of days. If you left a bottle of lemonade on top of the block of ice the bottle would sink in and get deliciously cold. We weren't rich but we had meat three times a day, even if it had to be rabbit. Before myxomatosis was introduced, the Australian rabbit was a lightly built racing model that made excellent food. Only in a protein-rich country like Australia could such a marvellous beast be looked down on. Left-over rabbit legs could be put in the ice-chest after dinner and eaten for breakfast next day. Surrounded with cold white fat, they looked like maps of Greenland and tasted like a dryad's inner thigh.

4 The World According to Garp

John Irving

In his mind's eye, Garp saw his mother, Jenny Fields, all in white, held up in the sky by the towering Roberta Muldoon. He did not know what it meant, but his vision of Jenny Fields raised above a crowd chilled him in the same way that the ambulance on the cover of *The World According to Bensenhaver* had chilled him. He began talking to Duncan, about anything at all.

Duncan began talking about Walt and the undertow – a famous family story. For as far back as Duncan could remember, the Garps had gone every summer to Dog's Head Harbor, New Hampshire, where the miles of beach in front of

Jenny Fields' estate were ravaged by a fearful undertow. When Walt was old enough to venture near the water, Duncan said to him – as Helen and Garp had, for years, said to Duncan – 'Watch out for the undertow.' Walt retreated, respectfully. And for three summers Walt was warned about the undertow. Duncan recalled all the phrases.

'The undertow is bad today.'

'The undertow is strong today.'

'The undertow is *wicked* today.' *Wicked* was a big word in New Hampshire – not just for the undertow.

And for years Walt reached out for it. From the first, when he asked what *it* could do to you, he had only been told that it could pull you out to sea. It could suck you under and drown you and drag you away.

It was Walt's fourth summer at Dog's Head Harbor, Duncan remembered, when Garp and Helen and Duncan observed Walt watching the sea. He stood ankle-deep in the foam from the surf and peered into the waves, without taking a step, for the longest time. The family went down to the water's edge to have a word with him.

'What are you doing, Walt?' Helen asked.

'What are you looking for, dummy?' Duncan asked him.

'I'm trying to see the Under Toad,' Walt said.

'The what?' said Garp.

'The Under Toad,' Walt said. 'I'm trying to *see* it. How *big* is it?'

And Garp and Helen and Duncan held their breath; they realized that all these years Walt had been dreading a giant *toad*, lurking offshore, waiting to suck him under and drag him out to sea. The terrible Under Toad.

Garp tried to imagine it with him. Would it ever surface? Did it ever float? Or was it always down under, slimy and bloated and ever-watchful for ankles its coated tongue could snare? The vile Under Toad.

Between Helen and Garp, the Under Toad became their code phrase for anxiety. Long after the monster was clarified for Walt ('Under*tow*, dummy, not Under Toad!' Duncan had howled), Garp and Helen evoked the beast as a way of referring to their own sense of danger. When the traffic was heavy, when the road was icy – when depression had moved in overnight – they said to each other, 'The Under Toad is strong today.'

'Remember,' Duncan asked on the plane, 'how Walt asked if it was green or brown?'

Both Garp and Duncan laughed. But it was neither green nor brown, Garp thought. It was me. It was Helen. It was the color of bad weather. It was the size of an automobile.

Family

1 The Rain Forest

Olivia Manning

5

Kristy realized that a new interest possessed the women at the Daisy, though they discussed it so cautiously she had no idea what it was. And she did not care. She was feeling her increasing weight and the humid heat was a burden to her. She was in a state of mental lethargy and physical well-being. Looking at herself in the glass, she smiled to see how she had changed. Ambrose had described her as 'small, dark, subtle, intelligent'. He was remembering her as she had been when he first saw her. She had been pale, over-thin and had looked delicate. Now her face had filled out and her complexion was brilliantly pink and cream. Her breasts, that had been too small, began to strain against her cotton shirts. Big, round, pink-cheeked, she looked a totally different person. She was turning into a mother. Mentally, too, she was melting into motherhood. Her emotions were becoming very tender. Remembering how she had found her mother weeping at the police-station, she now understood why she had wept. They had fought day in, day out: they had disagreed on every subject. At times Kristy had felt pure hatred for her mother and imagined herself hated in return. Yet they were one flesh. However outrageously Kristy behaved, she remained what she had been and always would be: part of her mother. She thought: 'I'll write and tell her that I understand' but from sheer lack of energy, she did not write.

She went once a week to see Mueller. At first Hugh had felt it was his duty to go with her but he was soon discouraged for the relationship between patient and gynaecologist was so warm, so intimate, he felt an extraneous third party. After three visits, he went no more.

On Mueller's advice, Kristy walked, each morning, for two or three miles. She would plod up to the plantations or go along the quay to the shore road and watch the flying-fish. Having done this, she could spend the rest of the day idle and thinking of meal-times. Previously a non-eater, she now ate ravenously. When she lay about in the salon or in her own room, she was poignantly conscious of the creature developing within her. She had decided not to return home until it was born. She would not risk the long, exhausting journey. But she still thought of it as her very own, inseparable from her however separated in space, and independent and unco-operative, it might one day become. It seemed to her – a fact she faced sometimes with joy, sometimes with irritation and a sense of revolt – that she would never be free again.

She had nothing to wear but an Arab skirt, bought in the harbour market, and a blouse to hide the gap at the waist-line. She could tell from glances in the salon that the progress of her pregnancy was being noted. It was noted most fequently by Mr Simpson who, whenever he caught her eye, parted his lips as though on the point of speech.

Mrs Axelrod occasionally slid her eye in Kristy's direction but looked the other way if Kristy met her glance. She had a new activity that increased her importance among her following. She was making, with an unusually large crochet-hook and some fine string, a circular table-cloth which she frequently spread out for the admiration of the others. It rapidly took on size so it was soon too big to display on the salon coffee-tables and had to be unrolled on the floor. Watching her as she crawled round it, flattening its uneven surface with the heel of her hand, Kristy thought: 'Poor old thing, what has she got in life?' Mrs Axelrod, unlike most of the other women who had children in England, was childless. When the talk was about schools, examinations or careers, she no longer ruled the conversation though, when possible, she gave advice as one who was likely to know more than the next woman. Still, she needed no one's pity. She observed her work with self-congratulating complacency and spoke of it in the same way. She was frequently asked how much bigger she planned to make it. Each time she considered the question anew, saying: 'I expect they'll have a sizeable place. They'll entertain in style. Big dinner parties: that sort of thing.'

2 The Right True End

Stan Barstow

NINE

At least I don't have to wait for trains nowadays, I tell myself as I slip on to the motorway and gently put my foot down. None of that Longford to Liverpool Street, Liverpool Street to Kings Cross, Kings Cross to Wakefield, Wakefield to Cressley and a bus out of town routine. I can travel door-to-door in my own good time, and as many or as few times as I wish.

I haven't been as often as I should, partly out of idleness, partly because the Old Lady has never really forgiven me for breaking up my marriage – though

Ingrid has been married again for some years now, as far as I know happily, to a chap who works in a bank – and my not 'settling down' again in her terms gives her every excuse to look askance at my way of life. If anything, my degree and my good job only make her more disappointed that I haven't found another wife and produced a couple of grandchildren to add to Bobby, and Jim's twin girls.

Why won't I conform, fit to pattern?

'Nay,' I can imagine her saying, 'he's got a grand job, and no worries about money, but he just doesn't seem to want to settle *down*.'

As though I were living in a tent and moving from town to town, job to job, as the whim took me.

The trouble is, I know what she means. I can't laugh it off because what she wants for me is what I want for myself. To her it's easier to find, that's all. You just work harder at it when you've got it; learn to be content; accept your lot. But I've been through all that. Oh, I'm no loner; my present life is not a pattern I've consciously created; it's something that's come about from living one day and then the next. I don't see it being like this for ever more. But I've not seen any alternative that's tempted me for longer than it's taken me to consider the hell of getting it wrong a second time.

Rosie, the Canadian girl who moved in with me for a couple of months, used to tell me there were no cast-iron certainties in this life, pronouncing it as the collected wisdom of her twenty-two years. I had to agree. She was near the end of her time in England when I met her and she finished her post-graduate course at London University and went home to Montreal. I think if I'd asked her to marry me she'd have stayed. Or am I flattering myself? Anyway, I didn't, and she left. I don't expect many relationships as good as mine and Rosie's. She stripped like the centre page of *Playboy*, her body drawing other men's eyes in a way that made me positively glow with the pleasure of temporary possession. She was lively, intelligent, shared a lot of my tastes, and was buoyantly accommodating between the sheets and on top of them. She made me laugh often and when she went I suddenly thought I would miss her like hell. But no, that faded soon enough, until I could think of her with sweet and gentle pleasure, and no regrets. So why couldn't what we had have been enough? Why didn't I accept all those pleasureable ingredients as being the best I was likely to find?

Damn it! I want something I can't bear to be without, because anything less must be in constant jeopardy.

With my petrol tank topped-up, I forge on. It's a dry clear night, which is one small blessing. Here, south of the Birmingham link, there's quite a lot of swift-moving heavy traffic on the road, and I'm up to eighty and passing it in the middle and third lanes before I realize that I'm going too fast, putting too much strain of concentration on someone who started out far from fresh. I pull over into the slow lane and ease off to sixty-five, letting who wants to pass me. My haste might be seemly but that's all that can be said for it. More sensible, I think, to have stayed put, where Chris could phone me with news. Because if the Old Lady is all that poorly they won't be letting anybody see her, and now I'm out of touch. I should at least have asked Chris where they'd taken her so that I could ring up for myself.

I switch on the radio and wind down the window as my eye-lids begin to droop, and suffer the inrush of cold air till my right hand goes nearly numb on the wheel. My privates feel heavy with my unshot load, on the edge of aching with the orgasm that first Miriam's response then Chris's phone call thwarted. Tenderness, Miriam wanted, tonight of all nights; Miriam who usually grabs sex like a kid stuffing its face with chocolates. Short, sharp and often is her usual style. Let's get it done with and then we can do it again. I've forgotten, of course, to get back that key. But it was no time to ask her for it, even if I'd remembered.

About the half-way point is the service area at Leicester Forest East, in my experience one of the few purporting to offer refreshment to the weary traveller along the motorways which doesn't put you off food altogether. God knows what foreign drivers make of them, faced with endless soggy chips, hot pies with crusts like wet cardboard and sausages overcooked and then kept warm till they're as hard as dog turds grilled by the sun. I pull in, park and go upstairs to the Buttery. There, over a cup of coffee, I can look out and see the headlights swooping on the carriageways.

My mother . . . Women are tougher than men. They outlive them. The world is full of widows. The Old Lady was all set to be one of them, soldiering on into her nineties, until she became a similar fixture to her great-grandkids. That's the thing about parents: they *are* fixtures, fixed always at the age they are now, changing only when your back's turned long enough. You can't remember what they were like when they were young, and you can't imagine how the world will close over them and carry on as before when they're gone.

3 Billy Liar

Keith Waterhouse

Lying in bed, I abandoned the facts again and was back in Ambrosia.

By rights, the march-past started in the Avenue of the Presidents, but it was an easy thing to shift the whole thing into Town Square. My friends had vantage seats on the town-hall steps where no flag flew more proudly than the tattered blue star of the Ambrosian Federation, the standard we had carried into battle. One by one the regiments marched past, and when they had gone – the Guards, the Parachute Regiment, the King's Own Yorkshire Light Infantry – a hush fell over the crowds and they removed their hats for the proud remnants of the Ambrosian Grand Yeomanry. It was true that we had entered the war late, and some criticized us for that; but out of two thousand who went into battle only seven remained to hear the rebuke. We limped along as we had arrived from the battle-field, the mud still on our shredded uniforms, but with a proud swing to our kilts. The band played 'March of the Movies'. The war memorial was decked with blue poppies, the strange bloom found only in Ambrosia.

I put an end to all this, consciously and deliberately, by going '*Da da da da da da da*' aloud to drive the thinking out of my head. It was a day for big decisions. I recalled how I could always cure myself when I got on one of those counting sprees where it was possible to reach three thousand easily without stopping: I would throw in a confetti of confusing numbers or, if they didn't help, half-remembered quotations and snatches of verse. '*Seventy-three. Nine hundred and six. The Lord is my shepherd, I shall not want, he maketh me to lie down. Four hundred and thirty-five.*'

It was a day for big decisions. I had already determined, more for practical reasons than out of any new policy, to clip the thumb-nail which I had been cultivating until it was a quarter of an inch long. Now, lying under the pale gold eiderdown, staring up at the crinoline ladies craftily fashioned out of silver paper and framed in passe-partout (*they* would be coming down, for a start) I began to abandon the idea of saving the clipping in an ointment box; I would throw it right away, without a backward glance, and from now on short nails, and a brisk bath each morning. An end, too, to this habit of lying in bed crinkling my toes fifty times for each foot; in future I would be up at seven and an hour's work done before breakfast. There would be no more breath-holding, eye-blinking, nostril-twitching, or sucking of teeth, and this plan would start tomorrow, if not today.

I lay in bed, the toe-crinkling over; now I was stretching the fingers of both hands to their fullest extent, like two starfish. Sometimes I got an overpowering feeling that my fingers were webbed, like a duck's, and I had to spread them out to block the sensation and prevent it spreading to my feet.

My mother shouted up the stairs: 'Billy? *Billy! Are* you getting up?' the third call in a fairly well-established series of street-cries that graduated from: 'Are you awake, Billy?' to 'It's a quarter past nine, and you can stay in bed all day for all I care', meaning twenty to nine and time to get up. I waited until she called: 'If I come up there you'll *know* about it' (a variant of number five, usually 'If I come up there I shall *tip* you out') and then I got up.

I put on the old raincoat I used for a dressing-gown, making the resolution that now I must buy a real dressing-gown, possibly a silk one with some kind of dragon motif, and I felt in my pocket for the Player's Weights. I was trying to bring myself up to smoke before breakfast but this time even the idea of it brought on the familiar nausea. I shoved the cigarettes back in my pocket and felt the letter still there, but this time I did not read it. '*He scribbled a few notes on the back of a used envelope.*' The phrase had always appealed to me. I had a pleasing image of a stack of used envelopes, secured by a rubber band, crammed with notes in a thin, spidery handwriting. I took the used envelope out of my pocket with the letter still in it and thought up some jottings. '*Calendars. See S. re job. Write Boon. Thousand??? See Witch re Captain.*' Most of these notes were unnecessary, especially the bit about seeing Witch re Captain; that, along with the calendars, always a part-time worry, and the other bit about seeing S. re job, had kept me awake half the night. As for Thousand??? this was a ghost of idle thinking, the last traces of a plan to write a thousand words each day of a public-school story to be entitled *The Two Schools at Gripminster.* Having conceived the plan in early August, I was already thirty-four thousand words behind on the schedule. There were long periods of time when my only ambition was to suck a Polo mint right through without it breaking in my mouth; others when I would retreat into Ambrosia and sketch out the new artists' settlement on route eleven, and they would be doing profiles of me on television, 'Genius – or Madman?'

I put the ballpoint away and shoved the envelope back in my pocket, and on the cue of cry number seven, by far my favourite ('Your boiled egg's stone cold and *I'm* not cooking another') I went downstairs.

4 The Human Factor

Graham Greene

After lunch Sarah took Sam into the garden along with Buller so as to leave Castle alone with his mother for a little while. That was the monthly routine. Sarah meant well, but Castle had the impression that his mother was glad when the private interview was over. Invariably there was a long silence between them while Mrs Castle poured out two more unwanted coffees; then she would propose a subject for discussion which Castle knew had been prepared a long time before just to cover this awkward interval.

'That was a terrible air crash last week,' Mrs Castle said, and she dropped the lump sugar in, one for her, two for him.

'Yes. It certainly was. Terrible.' He tried to remember which company, where . . . TWA? Calcutta?

'I couldn't help thinking what would have happened to Sam if you and Sarah had been on board.'

He remembered just in time. 'But it happened in Bangladesh, Mother. Why on earth should we . . .?'

'You are in the Foreign Office. They could send you anywhere.'

'Oh no, they couldn't. I'm chained to my desk in London, Mother. Anyway you know very well we've appointed you as guardian if anything ever happened.'

'An old woman approaching ninety.'

'Eighty-five, Mother, surely.'

'Every week I read of old women killed in bus crashes.'

'You never go in a bus.'

'I see no reason why I should make a *principle* of not going in a bus.'

'If anything should ever happen to you be sure we'll appoint somebody reliable.'

'It might be too late. One must prepare against simultaneous accidents. And in the case of Sam – well, there are special problems.'

'I suppose you mean his colour.'

'You can't make him a Ward in Chancery. Many of those judges – your father always said that – are racialist. And then – has it occurred to you, dear, if we are all dead, there might be people – out there – who might claim him?'

'Sarah has no parents.'

'What you leave behind, however small, might be thought quite a fortune – I mean by someone out there. If the deaths are simultaneous, the eldest is judged to have died first, or so I'm told. My money would then be added to yours. Sarah must have *some* relations and they might claim . . .'

'Mother, aren't you being a bit racialist yourself?'

'No, dear. I'm not at all racialist, though perhaps I'm old-fashioned and patriotic. Sam is English by birth whatever anyone may say.'

'I'll think about it, Mother.' That statement was the end of most of their discussions, but it was always well to try a diversion too. 'I've been wondering, Mother, whether to retire.'

'They don't give you a very good pension, do they?'

'I've saved a little. We live very economically.'

'The more you've saved the more reason for a spare guardian – just in case. I hope I'm as liberal as your father was, but I would hate to see Sam dragged back to South Africa . . .'

'But you wouldn't see it, Mother, if you were dead.'

'I'm not so certain of things, dear, as all that. I'm not an *atheist*.'

It was one of their most trying visits and he was only saved by Buller who returned with heavy determination from the garden and lumbered upstairs looking for the imprisoned Tinker Bell.

'At least,' Mrs Castle said, 'I hope I will never have to be a guardian for Buller.'

'I can promise you that, Mother. In the event of a fatal accident in Bangladesh which coincides with a Grandmothers' Union bus crash in Sussex I have left strict directions for Buller to be put away – as painlessly as possible.'

'It's not the sort of dog that I would personally have chosen for my grandson. Watchdogs like Buller are always very colour-conscious. And Sam's a nervous child. He reminds me of you at his age – except for the colour of course.'

'Was I a nervous child?'

'You always had an exaggerated sense of gratitude for the least kindness. It was a sort of insecurity, though why you should have felt insecure with me and your father . . . You once gave away a good fountain-pen to someone at school who had offered you a bun with a piece of chocolate inside.'

'Oh well, Mother. I always insist on getting my money's worth now.'

'I wonder.'

'And I've quite given up gratitude.' But as he spoke he remembered Carson dead in prison, and he remembered what Sarah had said. He added, 'Anyway, I don't let it go too far. I demand more than a penny bun nowadays.'

'There's something I've always found strange about you. Since you met Sarah you never mention Mary. I was very fond of Mary. I wish you had had a child with her.'

'I try to forget the dead,' he said, but that wasn't true. He had learnt early in his marriage that he was sterile, so there was no child, but they were happy. It was as much an only child as a wife who was blown to pieces by a buzz bomb in Oxford Street when he was safe in Lisbon, making a contact. He had failed to protect her, and he hadn't died with her. That was why he never spoke of her even to Sarah.

5 The Norman Conquests

Alan Ayckbourn

ANNIE: Yes.

NORMAN: I'll sit here, Shall I? All right if I sit here? Anybody any objections if I sit here? [*He is ignored.*] I'll sit here.

[NORMAN *sits at the head of the table.* SARAH *sits at the other end with* ANNIE *close to her, isolating* NORMAN. NORMAN *sits whistling.* REG *enters.*]

REG: [*cheerily*] Morning all.

NORMAN: Morning.

REG: [*his face falling*] Oh.

[REG *sits next to* SARAH. ANNIE *and* REG *have cereal.* SARAH *butters toast.*]

NORMAN: Well, you're a right cheery lot, aren't you? Look at you. A right cheery lot. Woo-hoo . . . hallooo . . . [*He waves at them.*]

SARAH: [*acid*] Nobody in this house is speaking to you ever again.

NORMAN: Oh, I see. I see. That's the way the Swiss rolls. I see. That's the way the apple crumbles, is it? Oh ho. That's the way the corn flakes . . . [*A pause. He ponders. Suddenly sharply*] Sarah! Be careful! The butter . . .

SARAH: [*alarmed*] What?

NORMAN: Ha-ha! You spoke to me. Caught you. Caught you. [*Pause.*] All right, I'll talk to myself then. [*Very rapidly, in two voices*] Hallo, Norman – good morning, Norman – how are you, Norman – I'm very well, Norman – that's good news, Norman –

ANNIE: Shut up, Norman.

NORMAN: Ha-ha! Caught you again. That's two of you. Just got to catch old Reg now. Two out of three. Just Reg left . . . [*slight pause*] Look out, Reg! [*No reaction.*] Ah – can't catch him that way. [*Sharply*] Hey, Reg! . . . oh well. If that's the way it is. Don't talk to me. I don't care. Doesn't bother me. I don't know why you're all being so unsociable. All right, I had a few drinks last night. What's wrong with that? Hasn't anyone round this table ever had a drink then? Come on, I don't believe it. You've had a drink haven't you, Reg? Ha-ha! Ha-ha! Caught you. You spoke.

REG: No, I didn't.

NORMAN: Ha-ha! Three to me. I've won. [*Pause*] Nothing wrong in a few drinks. Don't speak. I don't care. Going to be a pretty dull Sunday if we all sit in silence, I can tell you. Well, I'm not sitting in silence. I'll find something to do. I know, I'll go up and frighten Mother.

[SARAH *looks up sharply and gives him a terrible glare.*]

Ah-ha! Nearly got you again. Is it too much to ask for something to eat?

[*No response.*]

It's too much to ask for something to eat.

[*He gets up and moves down the table and takes the cereal bowl that* SARAH *isn't using.*]

May I borrow your bowl? That's awfully nice of you. And your spoon? Thank you. Now then, what shall I have? [*Examining cereal packets*] Puffa Puffa rice. Ah-ha . . . [*He returns to the top of the table, sits and fills his bowl.*]

No Sunday papers. Dear, dear. Ah, well I shall have to read my morning cereal . . . [*He laughs*] Cereal. Do we all get that? Apparently we don't. [*He reads. Suddenly, violently banging the table*] Stop!

[*The others jump involuntarily.*]

Stop everything. Listen. A free pair of pinking shears for only 79p and six Puffa Puffa tokens. Hurry, hurry, hurry. What's this? Is nobody hurrying? Do you mean to tell me that none of you want them? Where's the spirit of British pinking? Dead, presumably. Like my relations. [*He eats a handful of dry cereal thoughtfully*] Hang on, I've got another game. Mind reading. I'll read your minds. Now then, where shall we start? Sarah. Sarah is thinking – that noisy man up there should be home with his wife. What is he doing shattering the calm of our peaceful Sunday breakfast with his offers of reduced price pinking shears? Why is he here, shouting at us like this? Why isn't he at home, like any other decent husband, shouting at his wife? He came down here to seduce his wife's own sister. How low can he get? The fact that his wife's own sister said, at one stage anyway, that she was perfectly happy to go along with him is beside the point. The fact that little Annie here was perfectly happy to ditch old reliable Tom – without a second thought – and come off with me is beside the point. We won't mention that because it doesn't quite fit in with the facts as we would like them. And what is little Annie thinking, I wonder? Maybe furtively admiring my pyjamas, who knows? Pyjamas that could have been hers. With all that they contain. These nearly were mine. Or maybe she is thinking . . . Phew, that was a close shave. I could have been shacked up in some dreadful hotel with this man – at this very moment . . . what a lucky escape for me. Thank heavens, I am back here at home amidst my talkative family exchanging witty breakfast banter. Knowing my two-legged faithful companion and friend, Tom the rambling vet, is even now planning to propose to me in 1997 just as soon as he's cured our cat. Meanwhile, I can live here peacefully, totally fulfilled, racing up and down stairs looking after Mother, having the time of my life and living happily ever after until I'm fifty-five and fat . . . I'm glad I didn't go to that hotel. Well, let me tell you so am I. I wouldn't want a weekend with you, anyway. And I'll tell you the funniest thing of all, shall I? . . .

[ANNIE *gets up and runs out.*]

[*Yelling furiously after her*] I didn't even book the hotel. I knew you wouldn't come. You didn't have the guts.

[*A pause.*]

SARAH: You can be very cruel, can't you Norman?

[SARAH *goes out after* ANNIE.]

NORMAN: Oh, well. It's a bit quieter without those two. Hear yourself speak. Too damned noisy before. All that crunching of toast. Like a brigade of Guards marching on gravel. Well now, Reg –

[REG *chews glumly through his cereal.*]

[*Looking round the table*] Milk? Ah. [*He gets up.*] Sugar? [*He returns with these and sits. Pouring milk over his cereal*] Nice peaceful morning. Just the two of us and – hark! the soft crackle of my Puffa Puffa rice. 'Tis spring indeed. [*Slight pause.*] I suppose you think I'm cruel too, don't you? Well, I've damn good cause to be, haven't I? I mean, nobody's thought about my feelings, have they? It's all Annie – Annie – Annie . . . what about me? I was going to give her everything. Well, as much as I could. My whole being. I wanted to make her happy for a weekend, that's all. I wanted to give her . . . [*Angrily*] It was only for a few hours for God's sake. Saturday night, back on Monday morning. That was all it was going to be. My God! The fuss. What about your wife, Norman? What about my wife? Don't you think I'd take Ruth away, just the same? If she'd come. But she won't. She has no need of me at all, that woman, except as an emotional punch bag . . . I tell you, if you gave Ruth a rose, she'd peel all the petals off to make sure there weren't any greenfly. And when she'd done that, she'd turn round and say, do you call that a rose? Look at it, it's all in bits. That's Ruth. If she came in now, she wouldn't notice me. She'd probably hang her coat on me . . . It's not fair, Reg. Look, I'll tell you. A man with my type of temperament should really be ideally square jawed, broad shouldered, have blue twinkling eyes, a chuckle in his voice and a spring in his stride. He should get through three women a day without even ruffling his hair. That's what I'm like inside. That's my appetite. That's me. I'm a three a day man. There's enough of me in here to give. Not just sex, I'm talking about everything. The trouble is, I was born in the wrong damn body. Look at me. A gigolo trapped in a haystack. The tragedy of my life. Norman Dewers

– gigolo and assistant librarian. What's inside you, Reg? Apart from twelve bowls of cornflakes? What do you feel with Sarah? Do you sometimes feel like saying to her, no this is me. The real me. Look at me . . . [REG *finishes his cornflakes.*]

6 The Ginger Man

J. P. Donleavy

Raining outside. Cold morning. Felicity in her pram in the kitchen, wiggling a toothbrush in a jam jar. Marion standing against the mantelpiece in front of the black empty grate. Wearing slippers, wrapped in a blanket, her shanks showing. Just finished reading the letter, folding it carefully and slipping it back into its envelope.

I could tell there was trouble. I came down the stairs with my usual innocence and pain right smack into her silence which is the sign that she has a weapon. She stood there as if she were watching the groom saddle her horse. There was a smear of lipstick at the corner of her mouth, gave her a twisted smile. I thought for a second she was an Inca. She was quite polite when I asked her who the letter was from. She said simply, from your father.

'I'll get my glasses.'

'I'm afraid the letter is addressed to me.'

'What do you mean, you're afraid?'

'Just that. You're not going to read it.'

'Now just a minute, that letter is from my father and I intend to know what's in it.'

'And I intend you shan't.'

'Don't get snotty.'

'I'll be as snotty as I want. I no longer have to tolerate your nastiness.'

'What's this mumbo jumbo. Don't act as if you have a secret file on me.'

'I assure you it's not mumbo jumbo. I'm leaving this house.'

'Now look, Marion, I don't feel well. I'm not up to farting about at this godforsaken hour of the morning. Now just what the hell do you mean you're leaving this house?'

'Leaving this house.'

'There's a lease.'

'I know there's a lease.'

'For three years.'

'I know it's for three years.'

Marion's eyebrows raised. She kept reaching over her shoulder, pulling the blanket up. Sebastian stood in the doorway wearing a pair of purple pajamas, bright red slippers and a gray turtle necked sweater, its yarn unravelling, the string suspended behind him and disappearing up the stairs.

'Ah for Jesus sake, now let's not get started. I only want to know what you're talking about. You know, just for the sake of making things clear, I'll never get this damned exam if I have to face more misunderstanding. Now what is it? Has my father made you an offer of money or something?'

'You're not reading the letter.'

'All right. I'm not reading the letter. Now tell me, what the hell is this all about?'

'Your father is on my side.'

'Look Marion, all right. Now we know that you have everything your way. I know the drivel in that letter. Probably sent you a check.'

'As a matter of fact, he did.'

'Told you that I've always been a bastard.'

'Quite.'

'Expelled from schools.'

'Yes.'

'All right. What are you going to do?'

'Move from here, instantly.'

'Where?'

'I'm going to see an agent this morning.'

'What about the lease?'

'That's your doing.'

'You stupid bitch.'

'Go right ahead. Say anything you want. It matters nothing to me. By the way, you've left half my sweater on the stairs.'

'Now, Marion, let's understand each other. I don't feel that this fighting is going to get us anywhere.'

'It's certainly not going to get you anywhere.'

'Now look, how much is the check.'

'That's my business.'

'I've got to get my typewriter out of the pawn. I must have it for my notes.'

'Ha. Ha. Ha.'

Marion's mocking head back, disdainfully shutting eyes. The blue vein, handsome and large on the blonde throat. Pink slip and her shanks shifting the slippers, grinding the coal dust on the floor.

'Supposing I admit to a few indiscretions.'

'Indiscretions? That really is amusing you know.'

'Now that we have a chance to start over again.'

'We do, do we? O we. It's we now.'

'I'm thinking about the lease.'

'You signed it.'

Sebastian turned and went quietly up the stairs. Tip toe, tip toe. Dragging the wool string behind. Into the bedroom. Dropping the purples, pulling on the trousers. Tied a knot in the sweater. Put his sockless feet into shoes. A jacket for the respect that was in it. And my dear pair of golfing shoes. Pity, but must to the pawn. Ten and six for sure. Now my dear Marion, I'll give you a little something to think about.

In the toilet, Sebastian forced a board up from the floor. He hammered a nail through the lead pipe with the heel of his golfing shoe. He went quietly down the stairs. Marion saw him pass out the hall. The door squeaked shut.

I'll say one thing. She's not going to pull this stuff much longer. This is final. If she wants it this way, this way it shall be.

In this bitterness and hazy hatred. No cozy road to the swelled udders. This is at the midnight of everything. Because when I was living in America I had a lot of good things. I never had to think about hot water. I went to my club where it was running rampant.

Education

1 Schoolmaster

Yevtushenko

The window gives onto the white trees.
The master looks out of it at the trees,
for a long time, he looks for a long time
out through the window at the trees,
breaking his chalk slowly in one hand.
And it's only the rules of long division.
And he's forgotten the rules of long division.
Imagine not remembering long division!
A mistake on the blackboard, a mistake.
We watch him with a different attention
needing no one to hint to us about it,
there's more than difference in this attention.
The schoolmaster's wife has gone away,
we do not know where she has gone to,
we do not know why she has gone,
what we know is his wife has gone away.

His clothes are neither new nor in the fashion;
wearing the suit which he always wears
and which is neither new nor in the fashion
the master goes downstairs to the cloakroom.
He fumbles in his pocket for a ticket.
'What's the matter? Where is that ticket?
Perhaps I never picked up my ticket.
Where is the thing?' Rubbing his forehead.
'Oh, here it is. I'm getting old.
Don't argue auntie dear, I'm getting old.
You can't do much about getting old.'
We hear the door below creaking behind him.

The window gives onto the white trees.
The trees there are high and wonderful,
but they are not why we are looking out.
We look in silence at the schoolmaster.
He has a bent back and clumsy walk,
he moves without defences, clumsily,
worn out I ought to have said, clumsily.
Snow falling on him softly through silence
turns him to white under the white trees.
He whitens into white like the trees.
A little longer will make him so white
we shall not see him in the whitened trees.

2 The Chip-Chip Gatherers

Shiva Naipaul

Chapter Six

There was one fact around which Wilbert Ramsaran's life revolved and beside which nothing else mattered: the Ramsaran Transport Company. It was to provide him with his role and function in life. Of that, there could never be any serious doubt or question. From the earliest days it had been drummed into his head that nothing else was expected of him. 'I don't want you to come with any doctor stupidness to me,' Egbert Ramsaran had said. 'Leave that to Bholai. I not going to tolerate any nonsense from you. I sending you to school so that you could learn to read and write and add and subtract – especially add and subtract because that is what your life will be about. Nothing else! That was all I needed in my day so I don't see why it should be any different with you.'

Accordingly, operating on the instructions he had received, Wilbert neglected the frills of education and concentrated his efforts on mastering the arts of addition and subtraction; and learning to read and write tolerably well. These accomplishments successfully achieved, the education of Wilbert Ramsaran came to an effective end. School, as such, held no further interest for him. Wilbert did not seek the companionship of boys of his own age. He had nothing in common with most of them: their ambitions and general outlook were not his. His fate had already been decided and their competitive cleverness and passion for the frills of education irritated him. Nevertheless, he was acutely sensitive to their jibes and was quick to take offence at insults – real and imaginary. He was proud of his natural physical strength and was always ready to call on it to settle arguments.

Having fulfilled his father's commands, he seized every opportunity to absent himself from the irksome confinement of the classroom and to roam haphazardly around the seedier streets of Port-of-Spain to which he was irresistibly drawn. His teachers complained to Egbert Ramsaran. 'Your son does hardly ever be in school,' they said. 'At the rate he seem to be going he won't learn anything.' Egbert Ramsaran's response was disappointing. 'You try beating him?' 'We tried beat him,' they replied, 'but it don't seem to have any effect on him at all.' Egbert Ramsaran laughed. 'He could read and write?' 'Just about,' they said. 'And he could add and subtract?' 'Yes,' they said, 'He very bright in arithmetic.' 'Well then, I don't see what all the fuss is about. That is all I send him to school to learn in the first place. I don't care about nothing else. I wouldn't be surprised if he have more to learn from outside school than inside it.' 'If that is your attitude,' they said, 'we can't do nothing.'

The teachers gave up on Wilbert and he was permitted to come and go virtually as he pleased. The arrangement suited him.

3 Unreliable Memoirs

Clive James

Toys were scarce. A few crude lead soldiers were still produced so that children could go on poisoning themselves but otherwise there was almost nothing. It was a big event when my mother bought me a little painted red cow. Presumably it was English. I took it to school and lost it. Next day she came with me to school, wanting to find out what had happened to it. My carelessness with everything she bought me went on hurting her for years. She construed it, accurately, as ingratitude. From the sensitivity angle I was about as obtuse as a child can be. I was sensitive enough about myself, but that's a different thing.

School, passable for the first year, became unbearable in the second, when the kind Miss Dear was supplanted by a hard case called Miss Turnbull. Dark, cold and impatient, Miss Turnbull might have been the firm hand I needed, but already I was unable to cope with authority. I still can't today, tending to oscillate between nervous flippancy and overly solicitous respect. In those days, when I was about a third of my present height and a quarter of the weight, there was nothing to do except duck. I did everything to get out of facing up to Miss Turnbull. I had Mondayitis every day of the week. As my mother dragged me down the front path, I would clutch my stomach, cross my eyes, stick out my tongue, cough, choke, scream and vomit simultaneously.

But there were some occasions when I ended up at school no matter what I did. It was then revealed that I had Dropped Behind the Class. Words I could not recognize would come up on the spelling wheel. The spelling wheel was a thick card with a window in it and a cardboard disc behind. As you turned the disc, words appeared one at a time in the window. I remember not being able to pronounce the word 'the'. I pronounced it 'ter-*her*'. The class had collective hysterics. They were rolling around on the floor with their knees up. I suppose one of the reasons why I grew up feeling the need to cause laughter was perpetual fear of being its unwitting object.

From the start of Miss Turnbull's reign until the day we left Jannali, every morning I would shout the house down. For my mother, the path leading from the front porch to the front gate became a Via Dolorosa. My act reached ever new heights of extravagance. Either it worked or it didn't. If it didn't I would sit in school praying for the bushfires to come early and incinerate the place. If it did I would either hang around the house or go and play with Ron, a truant of my own age who lived next to Hally the butcher down near the station. Ron was a grub. I was always being warned off him because he was so filthy. He and I used to squat under his house tweaking each other's ding, watching each other pee, and so on. I can't remember it all now. I suppose I have repressed it. If there was any sexual excitement, it took the form of intense curiosity, just as I was curious about my mother when we were in the bath together. I remembered the shock of seeing Ray undressed. He looked as if he had a squirrel hanging there. I had an acorn.

4 The Natural Order

Ursula Bentley

Martin came to find me before I had finished. The school was now thudding with activity and I could see boys streaming like a lava flow out of the assembly hall and into classrooms.

'There you are,' said Martin. 'I thought you'd be at assembly.' He had evidently suffered a small disappointment.

'Sorry. Was I supposed to go? I just felt desperate to prepare myself somehow.'

'Doesn't matter. What have you got there? Umm, this for 3B? Yes, that should keep them quiet for a bit. Not nervous, are you?'

'Yes.'

'You won't have any trouble. And if you do, I'm in Upper 6th B. Punishment is swift and painful.'

'I haven't believed in corporal punishment up to now.' I also had an idea that committed socialists did not either, but perhaps Martin did not allow his political beliefs to interfere with professional ethics.

'We'll see how long that lasts. Come on.'

Martin carried the books and I trotted at his elbow as we threaded our way through the swarming corridors. I had not apprehended the scale of Catholic boyhood until that moment. Martin seemed to enjoy leading me protectively through the crush, the object of blatant curiosity on all sides, his Angel to my

Tobias. After what seemed indeed a journey of Biblical proportions we arrived at our destination, a classroom on the top floor of a corridor in the most remote wing of the school. The door stood open onto a scene of boyish pandemonium. As we entered a missile flew from one side of the class to the other. Then sudden silence as Martin was observed, broken by the scurrying of bodies to their desks.

'Who threw that book?' he asked, his jaws lightly grinding together. A moment's silence. Then a hand was slowly raised at the back of the class.

'Riccio, isn't it?'

'Yes, sir.'

'Stand up, you bastard.' The boy got to his feet, in no special hurry. He seemed to be going through the motions of a familiar routine. He was long, thin and sallow and the sleeves of his blazer were too short. He attempted a look of shifty defiance. 'Do you throw books across the room at home, Riccio?'

'No, Sir.'

'Then why do you think you can do it here?'

'Don't know, Sir.'

'Whom were you trying to hit?'

'Swarzenski, Sir.'

'So, you think books are for hitting people with, do you? It's true you're not likely to apprehend the contents any other way. Very well. Pick up the book and wait outside.'

The boy reluctantly did as he was told. I stood, quivering with fright, a few paces behind Martin. His anger was genuine and terrible to me, the more so as the Wrath of God act came as a shock after his genial behaviour up till then. And I had not previously envisaged respect for the written word taking quite such violent expression. Martin allowed a dramatic pause after the door had closed behind Riccio. Then he said, 'If I catch anyone else treating a book like that, that boy will carry the scars for the rest of his life. Is that understood?'

I felt eager to assure him that it would not be me, but the boys recognized a rhetorical question when they heard one, and kept their eyes down.

His tone brightened. 'Now, I've brought your new English teacher along. Miss Slade.' Thirty-three pairs of eyes were trained on me. I smiled. No one smiled back, so I was left stranded with the damn thing on my face. 'Miss Slade is from London. She's new to the school, of course, and I expect you to give her all the co-operation and respect you had for Mr Fallowfield. It's not easy to take over in the middle of term and I shall be taking a special interest in seeing how well, or how badly, you behave under the circumstances. I've told Miss Slade to send any trouble-makers direct to me.

'All right, Miss Slade, I'll leave them to you. Riccio will be back in a minute.'

'Thank you, Mr Lewis.'

The boys straggled to their feet as he left the room. 'Sit down,' I said.

'We usually say the prayer first, Miss,' said a well-groomed boy in the first row.

'The prayer? I'm afraid I don't know it. Can you start, please?'

'Yes, Miss. In the name of the Father and of the Son and of the Holy Ghost, Amen. Oh my God, I offer Thee this lesson –'

As the boys crossed themselves, Martin's muffled voice could be heard in the corridor. It was followed by the sound of the impact of a large textbook on Riccio's behind and his yelps of agony.

'– for Thy greater honour and glory. Accept it as an earnest of our –'

Howls.

'– love. Blessed Virgin Mary, save us. Blessed Ambrose Carstairs, pray for us. In the name of the Father and of the Son and of the Holy Ghost, Amen.'

'All right, thank you. Sit down.' Most of them had already done so, and were exchanging indignation over Martin's treatment of Riccio.

'That's enough talking,' I said. The noise level rose.

Riccio came back into the classroom. He had evidently been crying, and still gulped and snuffled in an attempt to control himself. He approached me, but looking at the floor.

'I'm sorry I'm late, Miss.'

'That's all right. Go and sit down.' My eyes must have betrayed my horror at the sight of what amounted to my first battered child. I felt outraged at having been exposed to such brutality. Not that my sympathies were especially with Riccio; even before being reduced to a pulp he had struck me as a repulsive type. But my feelings towards Martin had suffered a sea-change. Besides being distasteful, the incident had something ostentatious about it: I sensed that he had been pleased to have the opportunity of demonstrating his authority. The hostility now rippling through the class suggested that he had also buggered my chances of capturing the hearts of 3B. For them, I would probably always be the bitch who got Riccio creamed.

There was nothing I could do about that at the moment, however. Of greater note was restoring order. Most of the class was commiserating with Riccio, and quite a few were threatening colourful fates for Martin. Above the row I heard someone say, 'Shut up. She'll snitch on ya.'

'Don't care if she does.'

'That's enough talking,' I repeated.

A chihuahua of a boy in the first row looked up from doodling on his book cover. 'You'll have to shout louder than that, Miss.'

'I should knock a few of their heads together, Miss,' added the dapper boy beside him.

'That should not be necessary.' However, I felt slightly comforted at having established some sort of rapport with these two. They looked at me with friendly, laconic sympathy.

'Why don't you take the names, Miss?'

'All right.' I reached for the plan with the legend 3B inscribed at the top, under the name of the school and the crest of the local authority.

'Now I'm going to take your names, so pipe down,' I shrieked. There was a slight lowering of the noise level. 'All right, you at the back with the boiled sweet stuck to your collar, what's your name?'

There was laughter as he indignantly felt for the sweet and raised a threatening fist at a boy across the room.

'Cod,' he said, still disgruntled.

'Cod?' Is that your Christian name or your surname?' Again there was laughter. I was cheered by their willingness to be amused.

'Boiled Cod, Miss,' someone suggested.

'You shut your face, Rattray, or I'll break your head open,' responded Cod.

'Kindly address your remarks to me. Your full name, surname first.'

'Cod, Arthur.'

'Thank you. Next?'

'de Maria, Paolo.'

'Baxter, Elvis.'

'Gottfried, Richard.'

The roll-call took some time, accompanied as it was by continual back-chat, spontaneous humour, occasional threats of physical violence and sporadic attempts by me to conduct the exercise in silence. At the end I was exhausted. Surely I did not have to teach them as well? I got my two friends in the front row to distribute the books.

'While the books are being given out, would one of you please tell me what you did with Mr Fallowfield.'

This time the outburst of laughter all but threw me against the blackboard. Even Dapper and the Chihuahua paused in their duties to laugh.

'You name it, Miss' called Riccio, by now, unfortunately, restored to high spirits.

'Lay off it, she's blushing,' cautioned a kindly soul.

'I don't know what you're talking about. Er – Paton, can you please summarize your curriculum under Mr Fallowfield.'

Even as I spoke the words, the inappropriateness struck me with great force. I was horrified to feel wracked with the desire to laugh myself. Despite my feigned ignorance, I knew well enough that the *double entendres* referred to the fact that the late Mr Fallowfield had been a homosexual. In my position I could not, of course, be party to such jokes, but the boys felt no such restraint. When the hysteria had died down a little, Paton rose to his feet.

'He used to play with us, Miss,' he said, encouraged by the others.

'A play you mean? Which one? What was it called?'

'No – I mean games, Miss.'

'Oh, shut up and sit down. If you're all going to be so puerile about it I can find out from Mr Lewis.'

'He don't know half of it, Miss. Him and Mr Fallowfield were daggers drawn.'

'I said sit down. And all of you turn to page 43.' To my surprise some of them actually did. 'I'll read you the passage first, and then you can go over it again yourselves before we go on to the questions. Pay special attention to the sentence structure and the function of the imagery.'

'What's imagery, Miss?'

'Oh Lord. Just pay attention, then.'

5 The Malayan Trilogy

Anthony Burgess

'No,' said Boothby, '*don't* take a pew. Remain standing.'

'I take it I can stand at ease?' asked Crabbe.

'The time for bloody stupid little jokes is over,' said Boothby. 'You've had it now. I don't mind your ruining your own career, but when you try to ruin mine as well . . .'

'I still don't know what's happened,' said Crabbe. 'I admit that I wasn't there for the lunch and the Sports, but I did what I could. I rang up the office. It wasn't my fault if you didn't get the message.'

'The whole point is,' said Boothby, 'that you'd made up your mind to be away. You knew what was going to happen.'

'Did you know?'

'Don't be a bloody fool. Only you knew about it, and you knew about it because it was your idea. You instigated it.'

'I still don't know what happened.'

'I'll bloody well tell you what happened. There they all were, the Sultan and the Mentri Besar, the British Adviser, the crowd from K.L., God knows how much royalty from all over the Federation. And they'd played the State anthem, and everything was going all right and they announced the first track event.'

'Yes? And what happened?'

'You know damn well what happened. Nothing happened.'

'Nothing?'

'The little bastards just sat there. They damn well refused to take part in any single event. Except the juniors. So all we had was the egg-and-spoon race and the sack race and the bloody hop, step and jump. That was the Sports.'

'And did anybody do anything about it.'

'I screamed myself blue in the face. And then the Mentri Besar appealed to the Malay boys and quoted the Koran to them. And some of them looked a bit bloody sheepish.'

'I see. And who were the ringleaders?'

'How the hell do I know? All I know is that it was your idea.'

'In all seriousness, and keeping my temper, what makes you think so?'

'What makes me think so? I like that. Ever since you've been here you've been encouraging these boys to go against discipline. There was the business of that expulsion. And I was right about that and you damn well know I was right. But you told them I was wrong. I know all about it, don't think I don't. You told them I was a bloody tyrant. And you were behind that protest meeting when I caned those prefects. And when I docked that holiday because of the bad exam results. It's all come out. One or two of the prefects here had the bloody sense to realize which side their bread was buttered. I've heard all about you. I've heard it all. That lad you were down on, that Chinese lad you said was a bloody Communist, he's told me a few things.'

'Such as?'

'Such as that you're a bloody Communist sympathizer yourself. You had him in your flat and you as good as told him that Communism was right and that the British were wrong in not recognizing the Communist Party. Can you deny that?'

'I was trying to draw him out. I still maintain that he *is* a Communist, and if you look carefully you'll probably find that he's at the root of your trouble. I told you before, but you wouldn't do a thing about it.'

'This Chinese lad proved himself the best bloody prefect I've got. Yesterday it was him who was pleading with them, threatening them even. He was in tears. He said the school had been let down and I'd been let down and the cause of democracy had been let down. There. What have you got to say about that?'

'Only this. That you're too damned innocent to live.'

'Look here,' said Boothby, red and threatening, 'I'll tell you what's going to happen to you, Crabbe. You're being transferred, and with a bloody bad report, too. And at the end of this tour I think you'll find yourself out on your ear.'

'You know, Boothby, perhaps I'm really the innocent one. I just don't understand. I've done my best for these boys, I even thought some of these boys liked me. I thought that I was really getting somewhere with them.'

'Oh, you got somewhere with them all right. You staged a nice efficient revolt. You made me and everybody look a pack of bloody fools.'

'Boothby, I want you to believe me when I say that I had nothing to do with that business. Frankly, I've never liked you. I've always thought you were inefficient, autocratic, unsympathetic, the worst possible headmaster for a School like this. But never would I dream of doing anything disloyal, so . . .'

'Yes, I know exactly what you've thought about me. And I know exactly what you've been doing, day after day, in the classroom, on the sports field, in the dining-hall, at prefects' meetings. You've been turning them against me, and that means turning them against everything this School stands for. You've been a traitor. You are a traitor. And you'll get the reward of a bloody traitor, you just wait and see.'

'I'm sorry you feel like that, Boothby. Really sorry. You're doing me a very grave injustice.'

'You'd better look at this,' said Boothby. He handed over a typewritten sheet.

'This is a record of what you've been doing. This is a protest from one of the best boys this School's ever had.'

Crabbe read:

Dear Sir,

I hope you will forgive my writing to you like this, but I find that I am becoming increasingly disturbed by some of the things that Mr Crabbe, the History Master, is saying in class, especially about the running of the School. I know I speak for all the boys when I say that he should not say these things. He is speaking as though he should be running the School himself and is always criticizing the things that you, sir, do to make the School an efficient and happy School.

First he said the expulsion of Hamidin was wrong. Then he said it was wrong to cane prefects when they have done wrong. Then he said it was not right to deprive the School of a holiday when, as is well known, it was the only way to make the School realize that they must do better work in the examinations. Then he said that you, sir, did not listen fairly to the things the boys say when they come to see you. Also, I believe that Mr Crabbe has many wrong political ideas and talks about freedom and independence when he really means Communism.

One day he called me into his flat and asked me many questions. He seemed annoyed that I was trying to help the younger boys to see how wrong Communism is. He said to me as follows . . .

'All right,' said Crabbe. 'There's the evidence, a load of lies and half-truths. How long will it be, do you think, before my transfer comes through?'

'It's going to be bloody soon,' said Boothby. 'The sooner the better as far as I'm concerned.' At that moment the peon came in with the Sunday newspapers. Boothby scanned the front pages of the *Sunday Gazette* and the *Sunday Bugle* with grim concentration. 'There you are,' he said. 'All over the front page. If I had my way you'd be bloody well shot.'

Crabbe went out, feeling not in the least depressed. The thing was so thoroughly absurd; the truth would out, sooner or later. He felt clean with innocence, as though he had just showered. He got into his car and drove slowly back to Light House. Tomorrow he must do something about applying for a driving licence.

Love

1 Efuru

Flora Nwapa

CHAPTER ONE

They saw each other fairly often and after a fortnight's courting she agreed to marry him. But the man had no money for the dowry. He had just a few pounds for the farm and could not part with that. When the woman saw that he was unable to pay anything, she told him not to bother about the dowry. They were going to proclaim themselves married and that was that.

Efuru was her name. She was a remarkable woman. It was not only that she came from a distinguished family. She was distinguished herself. Her husband was not known and people wondered why she married him.

It was after the festival in which young men and young women looked for wives and husbands that Efuru first met Adizua. Adizua asked her to marry him and she agreed.

One moonlit night, they went out. They talked of a number of things, their life and their happiness. Efuru told him that she would drown herself in the lake if he did not marry her. Adizua told her he loved her very much and that even the dust she trod on meant something to him.

'But what about the dowry?' the woman asked.

'You will come to me on Nkwo day. Every place will be quiet that day being market day. Take a few clothes with you and come to me. We shall talk about the dowry after.' Efuru agreed and went home feeling very happy and light.

'It's late, Efuru, where are you coming from?' one of her cousins asked her as she was opening the gate of the compound.

'Don't you see the moon?'

'Is that the reason why you should come home so late? I shall tell your father. A young woman like you should not be out so late.'

'I don't care whom you tell.'

The next morning the cousin went to Efuru's father and told him that he had seen Efuru at a very late hour last night and when he asked her why she was so late, she was rude to him.

'My brother, help me to talk. I am tired of talking. I don't know what is wrong with young women of these days. I noticed that Efuru has been coming home late for quite some time. I asked her whom she was seeing so late and she said nothing. If her mother were alive, she would have known how to handle her.'

'Do you think there is a man in her life?'

'I think so, my brother. If the man wants to marry her, there is nothing wrong about that. The man should come and fulfil the customs of our people and marry her. But as it seems now I don't think the man in question wants to marry her. And that is dangerous. What if she gets pregnant? Who will look after her, now that her mother is dead?'

'I shall do my best to be of any help to you. I shall investigate.'

On Nkwo day when everybody had gone to the market, Efuru prepared herself. She had her bath very early in the stream. She took great care that morning over her appearance. Her father was now not at home. She took a few of her belongings and went to her lover's house.

The mother of the young man went to the market; when she returned she was surprised to see Efuru's clothes and a few other possessions in her son's room. The young man was quick to explain. He told his mother that Efuru was his wife. 'I have no money for the dowry yet. Efuru herself understands this. We have agreed to be husband and wife and that is all that matters.' The young man's mother was excited for her son had indeed made a good choice.

'You are welcome, my daughter. But your father, what will you say to him?'

'Leave that to me, I shall settle it myself.'

Efuru's father returned from the market and did not see his daughter. 'Perhaps she went to the stream,' he said to himself.

But Efuru did not return. Just when he was about to go to bed, he heard a knock at the door.

'Who is that?'

'It's a man. Open the door.'

'Oh, is that you, my brother? Did you see Efuru?'

'Efuru has run away to a young man. It is a shame. Our enemies will glory in this. This young man is nobody. His family is not known. Efuru has brought shame on us. Something must be done immediately to get her back.'

'What are we going to do, my brother?'

'We shall send our young men to go to the man's house. Efuru will be asked to come home with them. That's all.'

On the appointed day, the young men went to bring back their daughter who had brought so much disgrace to them. Immediately Efuru saw the men, she came out and greeted them.

'Welcome, my brothers. What good wind brings you here today. I hope all is well?'

'All is well, our daughter,' the men said.

'We have come for a business,' the spokesman added.

'We shall have kola before the business. It is a pity my husband is not at home. He went to the farm.'

Efuru brought two big kola-nuts. They were fit only for kings. She put them before the men, with some alligator pepper. The spokesman took one kola nut and blessed it. Then he broke it and gave the men.

Meanwhile, Efuru brought out a bottle of home-made gin – a very good one that had been in a kerosene tin for nearly six months.

'I am sure you will like this gin. Nwabuzo had it buried in the ground last year when there was rumour that policemen were sent to search her house. When the policemen left, finding nothing, Nwabuzo was still afraid and left in in the ground. A week later, she fell ill and was rushed to the hospital where she remained for six months. She came back only a week ago. So the gin is a very good one.'

The men enjoyed the drink very much. They finished the bottle and some of them were even tipsy.

'We shall go, our daughter,' the spokesman said. 'You seem to be happy here and we wonder why your father wants us to bring you back. We shall tell him what we have seen. But your husband must fulfil the customs of our people. It is very important. Our enemies will laugh at us. Tell your husband, he must see your father. Let him not be afraid.'

2 How Far Can You Go?

David Lodge

Dennis couldn't help wondering whether Lynn was sexually experienced or not. He presumed she must be, if even Catholic students were sleeping together these days, but he knew almost nothing about her private life, except that she was twenty-five, came from South Wales, and had a flat some miles from the factory. She alluded occasionally to attending evening classes for pottery, but otherwise seemed to have no social life. One day he commented on this enigma to a colleague, who said, 'Didn't you know? I thought it'd been all round the shop. She's got a kid.'

'A kid?'

'What they call a one-parent family, these days, isn't it? In other words, some bloke put her in the family way, and then scarpered.'

'Perhaps she didn't want to marry him,' said Dennis.

'Perhaps. Silly girl should've got it adopted, then. Nice girl like her could get married easy. But who'd take on some other bloke's little accident?'

The discovery gave Lynn a new interest and a new pathos in Dennis's eyes. At the same time it made her crush on him a more worrying responsibility. Sometimes he wondered if it would not be kinder to get Lynn transferred to another job, even another factory, so that she could shake off her infatuation and perhaps meet some decent fellow who would be glad to marry her and give the child a father. But he hesitated and procrastinated, because he was unwilling to seem cruel in order to be kind, and because, in truth, he couldn't bear the prospect of parting from her. Then, at Christmas, their relationship changed decisively.

On Christmas Eve, work stopped on the shopfloor and in the stores and offices at midday, and a kind of serial party began, made up of lots of little parties, stretching round the factory like a paper-chain, with a great deal of drinking and seasonal fraternization between management and workers. Dennis did his bit in this respect, touring the different departments with a pocketful of cigars and taking a drink with each group of merrymakers. An atmosphere of boozy bonhomie and tawdry licence spread through the buildings. In the corridors Dennis crunched crisps and broken glass underfoot, skirted couples kissing greedily, mouth on mouth, still holding unfinished drinks and smouldering cigarettes in their outstretched hands, and heard behind the doors of the women's toilets the sound of young girls unaccustomed to liquor moaning and being sick. In the corner of one of the stores a woman packer, her face a raddled, grinning mask of powder and lipstick, was doing high kicks on a table, urged on by a rhythmically clapping crowd. It was the same every year at this season, one afternoon on which the accumulated repressions and frustrations of the rest of the year were discharged in a squalid orgy, the memory of its excesses being quickly buried in the stupor of a domestic Christmas. Usually Dennis merely tolerated the custom with a skin-deep show of party spirit, but today he felt genuinely excited. A project was forming in his head and would not be removed: under cover of this feast of misrule he could safely give Lynn a kiss, something, he realized, he had been wanting to do for some time. There would be nothing odd or untoward about such a gesture – on the contrary, bosses were kissing their secretaries all over the factory. Lynn could not imagine that he meant by it anything more than a friendly sign of affection, nor would it give scandal if they were observed. The more he thought about this idea, and the more nips of scotch he took on his tour of the factory, the more excited Dennis became, and as he approached his own department again he was gripped by a hollow, breathless feeling of erotic expectation more intense than anything he had felt in many years.

'Give us a kiss, then, Dennis!'

Doreen Wills, from Personnel, normally the hardbitten career woman incarnate, was ogling him from the door of the hospitality room, a glass in her hand and a paper hat askew on her upswept hairdo. She pointed upwards to a sprig of mistletoe pinned to the door frame. He fave her a perfunctory peck on the cheek, but she twisted her face round to glue her lips to his. 'Happy Christmas, Dennis, darling,' she said, breathing gin and sweet vermouth into his face. He responded absently, looking over her shoulder into the room where an impromptu disco was in progress. 'You know, I could really fancy you, Dennis,' said Doreen. 'Come and have a dance.'

'Sorry, Doreen, I don't go in for that kind of dancing,' he said. 'Have you seen Lynn anywhere?'

'Ah! Want to get her under the mistletoe, eh?'

'No, just got some work to finish off,' he lied, nettled by the shrewdness of her guess.

'For Christ's sake, Dennis, it's Christmas Eve! Anyway, I think she's gone home.'

'Home?' Dismayed, Dennis rushed off to Lynn's office. It was empty, and her coat had gone from its hanger behind the door. Angrily Dennis kicked this door shut, cutting off the sounds of carousing, and strode into his own office by the communicating door. Lynn, dressed in her outdoor clothes, looked up from behind his desk.

'Oh,' she said. 'I was just leaving you a card.' She held out a Christmas card to him like an alibi. He approached her and took it across the desk, in a queer reversal of their usual roles. 'It's very nice,' he said, glancing at it. 'Thank you.'

'I had a job getting a religious one,' she said. Then, leaning forward to peer at him, 'You've got lipstick all over your face.'

'Doreen Wills caught me under the mistletoe.'

'Lucky you,' she said drily. Her back was to the fading light of the December afternoon and he could not discern the expression on her face as she spoke.

'Unlucky, you mean.' He rubbed furiously at his mouth with the back of his hand.

'Don't do that, you'll just make it worse. Here, have a Kleenex.' She rummaged in her handbag.

'Pity we don't have a bit of mistletoe in here,' he said, attempting a light-hearted tone that came out as a strangled croak.

She looked up quickly. 'I'll remember to get some next year, then,' she said, holding out the tissue.

His hand closed over hers and pulled her gently forwards over the desk. 'I can't wait that long,' he said, 'to wish you a happy Christmas.' Supporting herself with her free hand, Lynn turned her cheek to receive his kiss. He had forgotten how soft a young girl's skin could be. 'That wasn't much of a kiss,' he said, keeping hold of her hand. 'Come round here.'

She shook her head.

'Please.'

'You come, if you want to,' she whispered.

Without letting go of her hand, as if performing some stately dance, he stepped round the end of the desk and drew her into his arms.

What followed took Dennis completely by surprise. He had had in mind a single, wistful kiss, a tender but decorous embrace that would convey his appreciation of Lynn and his affection for her, but at the same time confirm their mutual awareness of the circumstances that made any deeper relationship impossible. Lynn, however, clung to him as if she would never be prised loose, she flattened herself against him like a climber marooned on a cliff-face, she shuddered in his arms and sighed and moaned and ran her fingers through his hair and thrust her tongue between his teeth as if she wanted to climb inside his mouth and wriggle down his throat. Dennis's feeble lust was soon swamped by this demonstration. He was appalled by the intensity of the passion he had aroused, and daunted by the task of seeming equal to it. At last Lynn peeled her lips from his, sighed and nestled against his shoulder. Dennis, stroking her back as if comforting a child, stared past her head at the dusk gathering over the company car park. What now, he thought, what now? What does one do next? What does one say? There was nothing he could say, he realized, after trying out a few phrases in his head, that wouldn't sound either coldly dismissive or recklessly committing. It seemed to Dennis that a stark choice already stared him in the face between being a cowardly prig or an unfaithful husband; that, incredible as it seemed, one kiss had tumbled him irretrievably into a maelstrom of tragic passion and insoluble moral dilemmas.

'Shall I take you home?' he said at last. It was the most neutral thing he could think of, but the way Lynn nodded agreement immediately convinced him that, without intending it, he had sealed some sexual contract with her in the code which governed such matters.

In the car, neither of them spoke, except for her to give, and him to acknowledge, directions. Dennis drove like an automaton. He felt deprived of free will, as if the wheels of his car were locked into grooves carrying him inexorably towards adultery. He felt no excitement or lust, only a sense of doom and a fear that he would fail sexually, humiliating both of them.

He stopped the car outside a semi-detached Victorian villa. 'Will you come in?' Lynn said. It did not seem to Dennis that she meant it as a real question or that he had a real choice. He followed her into the ground-floor flat. There was a pushchair in the hall. 'I suppose you know I've got a little boy?' she said.

'I heard rumours,' he said. 'I didn't like to pry.' The sight of the pushchair had given him hope of a reprieve. 'Where is he now?'

'I've got a friend who collects him from the nursery. She keeps him till I call.'

The main room in the flat was furnished as a bed-sitting room. Lynn lit the gas fire, took off her coat, and flopped down on the divan bed. 'Too much Cyprus sherry,' she said, closing her eyes.

Dennis stooped over her, hopeful again. 'Are you all right?'

She put her arms round his neck and pulled him down beside her. Dennis stroked her breasts through the woollen dress she was wearing, put his hand under her skirt and slid it up over legs glazed in nylon tights. Now that he could see no way of avoiding the sexual act, he was impatient to get it over. 'Why don't you take this off?' he said, plucking at her dress; and sat up himself to take off his jacket, tie, shoes.

This cannot be happening, he thought. Behind him, Lynn said: 'Have you got something?'

'What?'

'You know . . .'

Dennis stopped in the act of undoing his belt, and turned to face her. She was still fully dressed, her skirt up round her thighs. 'Aren't you on the Pill, then?'

'No. Why should I be?'

'I don't know . . . I just thought . . .'

'I haven't got a fella, you know. And I don't go in for one-night stands.'

'I'm sorry, Lynn.' Red with embarrassment, he began to do up his belt, put on his shoes, his tie, his jacket. When he was dressed, he turned to her. She had not moved. He pulled down the hem of her skirt. 'Can we try and forget this ever happened?' he said.

'No,' she said.

He made a helpless shrugging gesture. 'Can we have a cup of tea, then?'

3 The Heart of the Matter

Graham Greene

'Let Freddie in,' the voice wheedled. 'Be a sport, Helen. Only Freddie Bagster.' The man was a little drunk.

She stood pressed against him with her hand on his side. When the sound of Bagster's feet receded, she raised her mouth and they kissed. What they had both thought was safety proved to have been the camouflage of an enemy who works in terms of friendship, trust, and pity.

2

The rain poured steadily down, turning the little patch of reclaimed ground on which his house stood back into swamp again. The window of his room blew to and fro: at some time during the night the catch had been broken by a squall of wind. Now the rain had blown in, his dressing-table was soaking wet, and there was a pool of water on the floor. His alarm clock pointed to 4.25. He felt as though he had returned to a house that had been abandoned years ago. It would not have surprised him to find cobwebs over the mirror, the mosquito-net hanging in shreds and the dirt of mice upon the floor.

He sat down on a chair and the water drained off his trousers and made a second pool around his mosquito-boots. He had left his umbrella behind setting out on his walk home with an odd jubilation, as though he had rediscovered something he had lost, something which belonged to his youth. In the wet and noisy darkness he had even lifted his voice and tried out a line from Fraser's song, but his voice was tuneless. Now somewhere between the Nissen hut and home he had mislaid his joy.

At four in the morning he had woken. Her head lay in his side and he could feel her hair against his breast. Putting his hand outside the net he found the light. She lay in the odd cramped attitude of someone who has been shot in escaping. It seemed to him for a moment even then, before his tenderness and pleasure awoke, that he was looking at a bundle of cannon fodder. The first words she said when the light had roused her were, 'Bagster can go to hell.'

'Were you dreaming?'

She said, 'I dreamed I was lost in a marsh and Bagster found me.' He said, 'I've got to go. If we sleep now, we shan't wake again till it's light.' He began to think for both of them, carefully. Like a criminal he began to fashion in his own mind the undetectable crime: he planned the moves ahead: he embarked for the first time in his life on the long legalistic arguments of deceit. If so-and-so . . . then that follows. He said 'What time does your boy turn up?'

'About six I think. I don't know. He calls me at seven.'

'Ali starts boiling my water about a quarter to six. I'd better go, my dear.' He looked carefully everywhere for signs of his presence: he straightened a mat and hesitated over an ashtray.

Then at the end of it all he had left his umbrella standing against the wall. It seemed to him the typical action of a criminal. When the rain reminded him of it, it was too late to go back. He would have to hammer on her door, and already in one hut a light had gone on. Standing in his own room with a mosquito-boot in his hand, he thought wearily and drearily. In future I must do better than that.

In the future – that was where the sadness lay. Was it the butterfly that died in the act of love? But human beings were condemned to consequences. The responsibility as well as the guilt was his – he was not a Bagster: he knew what he was about. He had sworn to preserve Louise's happiness, and now he had accepted another and contradictory responsibility. He felt tired by all the lies he would some time have to tell: he felt the wounds of those victims who had not yet bled. Lying back on the pillow he stared sleeplessly out towards the grey early morning tide. Somewhere on the face of those obscure waters moved the sense of yet another wrong and another victim, not Louise, nor Helen. Away in the town the cocks began to crow for the false dawn.

4 Sentence of Death

Terry Morgan

There was this bloke sitting at his bench at work one day when he came all over funny, so he got up and went to see the works doctor, who examined him thoroughly.

'Listen, Mr Murphy', the doctor said. 'I'm afraid I've got some very bad news for you. As far as I am able to judge, you've got about four hours to live.'

'What?' said the man. 'I don't believe it.'

'Sorry, Mr Murphy' the doctor said, 'But that's what my tests show.'

'I'd better go home and tell the missus about it, then,' said Murphy, shaken.

'Yes, I suppose the firm'll give you the afternoon off under the circumstances.'

The unfortunate victim went home. 'Listen, love,' he told his wife. 'I've only got four . . . well, say three and three-quarter hours to live.'

'Dear me,' she said. 'That's a blow. I thought we might go to my mother's on Saturday. Well, never mind. What do you want to do with your final hours, love?'

The man eyed his wife up and down. 'Let's go upstairs,' he said.

Half an hour later they were back in the kitchen. 'Three and a quarter hours left,' she said. 'What would you like to do next?'

Murphy considered. 'Make me,' he decided, 'a big juicy sirloin steak, very well done, with chips, petit pois, grilled mushrooms, and tomatoes, cheese and biscuits to follow and a half bottle of Medoc.'

'O.K. Bernie. I think we've got one of them left,' she said. 'Won't be long.'

She cooked the steak with all the trimmings and watched as he tucked into it. When he put his glass down for the last time she said, 'Two and a quarter hours to go, love. What do you want to do next?'

Murphy took a deep breath. 'Come back upstairs,' he said.

Half an hour later they were back in the living room. 'Well,' said Mrs Murphy, 'you've still got one and three-quarter hours to kill. Oh, sorry, love, I didn't mean it like that.'

'Never mind,' he said. 'I think I'd like a drink now. Get that bottle of brandy your dad gave me at Christmas and I'll polish that off.'

'Yes, love,' said his wife, and watched as he drank the whole bottle off. 'What do you want to do for your last hour and a quarter then?' she demanded.

'Lesh go back upstairsh,' he mumbled.

When they returned to the living room there were only fifty minutes to go. 'What now, angel?' she asked.

'Go to the pub,' he ordered, 'and get me a couple of foaming pints of creamy draught Guinness. If you have to go out, you might as well do it on the best drink there is.'

'Yes dear,' she said, and set off.

It didn't take our hero long to drink the delightful brew down when she came back.

'Well, my love,' his wife asked. 'What do you want to do for the last half hour on earth?'

'Let's go back upstairs,' he said.

'Oh aye,' she said. 'It's all right for you, but I've got to get up in the morning.'

5 My Name Blew Like a Horn Among the Payira

Okot P'Bitek

I was made chief of girls
Because I was lively,
I was bright,
I was not clumsy or untidy,
I was not dull,
I was not heavy and slow.

I did not grow up a fool
I am not cold
I am not shy
My skin is smooth
It still shines smoothly in the moonlight.

When Ocol was wooing me
My breasts were erect.
And they shook
As I walked briskly,
And as I walked
I threw my long neck
This way and that way
Like the flower of the *lyonno* lily
Waving in a gentle breeze.

And my brothers called me *Nya-Dyang*
For my breasts shook
And beckoned the cattle,
And they sang silently:

Father prepare the kraal,
Father prepare the kraal,
The cattle are coming.

I was the Leader of the girls
And my name blew
Like a horn
Among the Payira.
And I played on my bow harp
And praised my love.

Ocol, my husband,
My friend,
What are you talking?
You saw me when I was young.
In my mother's house
This man crawled on the floor!

The son of the Bull wept
For me with tears,
Like a hungry child
Whose mother has stayed long
In the simsim field!

Every night he came
To my father's homestead,
He never missed one night
Even after he had been beaten
By my brothers.

You loved my giraffe-tail bangles,
My father brought them for me
From the Hills in the East.

The roof of my mother's house
Was beautifully laced
With elephant grass;
My father built it
With the skill of the Acoli.

You admired my sister's
Colourful ten-stringed loin beads;
My mother threaded them
And arranged them with care.

You trembled
When you saw the tattoos
On my breasts
And the tattoos below my belly button;
And you were very fond
Of the gap in my teeth!

My man, what are you talking?
My clansmen, I ask you:
What has become of my husband?
Is he sufferng from boils?
Is it ripe now?
Should they open it
So that the pus may flow out?

I was chief of youths
Because of my good manners,
Because my waist was soft.
I sang sweetly
When I was grinding millet
Or on the way to the well
Nobody's voice was sweeter than mine!
And in the arena
I sang the solos
Loud and clear
Like the *ogilo* bird
At sunset.

Now, Ocol says
I am a mere dog
A puppy,
A little puppy
Suffering from skin diseases.

Ocol says
He does not love me any more
Because I cannot play the guitar
And I do not like their stupid dance,
Because I despise the songs
They play at the ballroom dance
And I do not follow the steps of foreign songs
On the gramophone records.
And I cannot tune the radio
Because I do not hear
Swahili or Luganda.

What is all this?

My husband refuses
To listen to me,
He refuses to give me a chance.
My husband has blocked up my path completely.
He has put up a road block
But has not told me why.
He just shouts
Like house-flies
Settling on top of excrement
When disturbed!

My husband says
He no longer wants a woman
With a gap in her teeth,
He is in love
With a woman
Whose teeth fill her mouth completely
Like the teeth of war-captives and slaves.

Society

1 The Happy Haven
John Arden

PHINEUS:
I'm an old old lady
And I don't have long to live.
I am only strong enough to take
Not to give. No time left to give.
I want to drink, I want to eat,
I want my shoes taken off my feet.
I want to talk but not to walk
Because if I walk, I have to know
Where it is I want to go.
I want to sleep but not to dream
I want to play and win every game
To live with love but not to love
The world to move but me not move
I want I want for ever and ever.
The world to work, the world to be clever.
Leave me be, but don't leave me alone.
That's what I want. I'm a big round stone
Sitting in the middle of a thunderstorm.
There you are: that's true.
That's me. Now: you.

2 The Rabbits Who Caused All the Trouble

James Thurber

Within the memory of the youngest child there was a family of rabbits who lived near a pack of wolves. The wolves announced that they did not like the way the rabbits were living. (The wolves were crazy about the way they themselves were living, because it was the only way to live.) One night several wolves were killed in an earthquake and this was blamed on the rabbits, for it is well known that rabbits pound on the ground with their hind legs and cause earthquakes. On another night one of the wolves was killed by a bolt of lightning and this was also blamed on the rabbits, for it is well known that lettuce-eaters cause lightning. The wolves threatened to civilize the rabbits if they didn't behave, and the rabbits decided to run away to a desert island. But the other animals, who lived at a great distance, shamed them, saying, 'You must stay where you are and be brave. This is no world for escapists. If the wolves attack you, we will come to your aid, in all probability.' So the rabbits continued to live near the wolves and one day there was a terrible flood which drowned a great many wolves. This was blamed on the rabbits, for it is well known that carrot-nibblers with long ears cause floods. The wolves descended on the rabbits, for their own good, and imprisoned them in a dark cave, for their own protection.

When nothing was heard about the rabbits for some weeks, the other animals demanded to know what had happened to them. The wolves replied that the rabbits had been eaten and since they had been eaten the affair was a purely internal matter. But the other animals warned that they might possibly unite against the wolves unless some reason was given for the destruction of the rabbits. So the wolves gave them one. 'They were trying to escape,' said the wolves, 'and, as you know, this is no world for escapists.'

Moral: Run, don't walk, to the nearest desert island.

3 The Interpreters

Wole Soyinka

The ambassador approached the Faseyis accompanied by a waiter bearing a trayload of champagne. Monica shook her head, and already Faseyi looked displeased. The ambassador was hospitably incredulous. 'But don't you drink at all, Mrs Faseyi?' 'No, only the occasional palm wine when our steward feels kindly towards us.' The ambassador laughed and gestured regretfully. 'I am so sorry, I really wish we had palm wine.'

One of the waiters was passing with more champagne and overheard. Faseyi had wandered off to seek the Master of Presentations; when he returned, Monica had a glass of palm wine in her hand, and a colleague of Faseyi was asking, 'What have you got there, Monica? Mist alba?'

'Where did you get that?' Faseyi shouted.

'One of the stewards brought it. He overheard us talk about palm wine and went to fetch it from his house. Wasn't that sweet of him?'

Faseyi went scrambling towards Bandele. 'You see, she has begun again.'

Bandele wore his mask of infinite patience. 'What has she done now?'

'It was bad enough to refuse the champagne, although mind you I just don't see any necessity for it. After all, how many of these women here touch their drink? They just hold the glass in their hand to be sociable, what is wrong with that?'

Kola murmured, 'Nothing, nothing, I'm sure.'

Faseyi looked at him with love and gratitude. 'But you see, that isn't all. She wasn't satisfied with that. She had to go and ask for palm wine at a cocktail reception. Have you ever heard such a thing? For palm wine!'

Bandele's grave aspect consoled him not at all.

'If she were a bush-girl from some London slum I could understand. But she is educated. She has moved in society. Why does she have to come and disgrace me by drinking palm wine?'

'Oh,' Kola looked concerned. 'You mean she even got it?'

Faseyi spun round. 'Look at her if you don't believe me. There she is over there, drinking palm wine if you please. And someone even came along as I saw her, and I bet he is spreading the story all over the place already.'

'Oh, he may not know it was palm wine.'

'He did. He was even sneering. Is that mist alba? That's what he said.'

'You should have said yes,' Kola told him. 'After all it would be more understandable that your wife was taken suddenly ill and had to have some mist alba.'

'Yes . . . I suppose so . . . I suppose so. I should have thought of it. But the trouble is Monica. She would have made some careless slip and given herself away. Look, Bandele, be a friend. If you hear any adverse comments, let me know, will you. Much better if one knew what people are saying in time, then one can do something about it. And also . . .' Faseyi drew closer and whispered, 'about her dress.'

Bandele said, 'What are you talking about?'

'Don't you see she is improperly dressed?'

'I hadn't noticed.'

In Faseyi's eyes a sudden gleam of hope. 'You mean you hadn't? Well that's a relief, perhaps most people won't either.'

'I am afraid you are wrong,' Kola said.

'Oh. So you've noticed.'

Kola improved on it. 'Not me. I don't know much about clothes. But I heard a group over there commenting on her.'

Turning to Bandele, 'You see!'

'I wouldn't pay much attention,' Kola continued. 'You get these spiteful types everywhere, and those ones were' – and a doleful shake of the head – 'anyway I don't need to tell you. You know how catty people can be.'

'No, no, it's not cattiness. They are quite right. Look, what did they say exactly?'

Bandele interfered and manoeuvred Faseyi away and towards his wife. They had hardly come to Monica before Faseyi burst out 'You see how conspicuous you've made us? Look around and see for yourself. Even those in native dress are wearing gloves.'

4 Close Encounters of the Third Kind

Steven Spielberg

TWENTY-SIX

As Roy clambered down the edge of the mountain, he noticed that the display was over. As though some signal had been given, all the objects flew off into the night.

Now in the background, coming out of the low clouds, a hundred points of light flared up around the entire twenty-mile perimeter of the box canyon. Although these light points were hovering at least ten miles away, Neary could tell they were large nuts and bolts vehicles, just hanging there, seeming to guard the perimeter of the base. Now they rose up higher in the sky and dimmed their lights. Roy could barely make out the black shapes behind the glow. It was very eerie.

Things got stranger still.

Down in the stadium, everyone was now exhausted. They were out of breath, picking themselves and their equipment up, brushing off their clothes. Scientists or not, they had all been going through a total culture shock, and each man was trying to handle it, deal with it.

There was no conversation. The wind had dropped off completely now, and the silence was total.

Neary had kept coming all this time and was now on the floor of the mountain, edging his way toward the perimeter of the base when something made him stop and look up.

From behind the mountain and from inside a cloud, something began coming out of the cloud that was completely black. It was not only black but it was huge. So huge that Roy could not comprehend its size. As the huge black shape came over the top of the mountain, blotting out the moon and casting a shadow that crawled over everybody in the canyon, Neary thought he was going to pass out.

Inside the base, the master of ceremonies murmured 'Oh, my God!' and fell to his knees.

'Holy shit!' Laughlin exclaimed, not hearing himself.

Lacombe stared transfixed. '*Mon Dieu*!' he said, realizing that if they could measure this shape, this thing, that it would be over a mile wide and the length of it, covering the entire sky, was still unknown because the end of it was not in sight.

Suddenly it turned on. A surgical sliver of light circumscribed the underside of the thing, and then something opened – some round circle of light exploded, like a corona of light.

It was the size of a city, Neary thought. Indianapolis. No, bigger. Detroit. The top of it looked like an oil refinery, with huge tanks and pipes and blazing fires and working lights everywhere. The phantom mass, sliding across the canyon, seemed somehow old and dirty. It looked junky, like an old city or an immense old ship that had been sailing the skies for hundreds, thousands, millions of years. Neither Roy nor any of the scientists or technicians – or anyone else on earth, for that matter – had ever seen or even imagined anything like it.

As it came over the base, a huge explosion of light flared out behind it and separated into what looked like a thousand brilliant fireflies, except that each 'firefly' was a small (by comparison) vehicle acting like a tugboat. Each 'tugboat' flashed different colours and the thousand of them together formed a scaffold of many-coloured lights onto which the phantom mass – two miles long and a mile wide – seemed to settle. The mass made a slight list as the scaffold – crossbeams blinking colours – escorted it to a landing area of its own far downfield.

Neary had vaulted over the six-foot retaining wall and was now wedged in among the technicians and scientists, all of whom were simply stunned by what they were seeing.

The scaffolding guided the mass down, squishing and shattering about a mile of the landing coordinate lights. It was so big that as it settled the leading edge of the mass formed a roof over the top of the entire camp.

The mass had created its own negative gravity field, and within a moment everyone and everything became about forty per cent weightless. Somehow it cheered everyone up. They started bouncing and cavorting buoyantly in the air, some of the more athletic doing cartwheels and somersaults, hanging in the air like Dr. J., their colleagues in jumpsuits sliding and bouncing beneath them with their cameras, snapping pictures of the whole incredible thing.

After the mass was down, the team around the synthesizer individually and collectively felt very faint. They were experiencing the essence of culture shock, despite the years of anticipation and preparation for just this moment.

Lacombe and the Team Leader were the first to recover partially. They decided to move the synthesizer, which was mounted on casters, closer to the mass. After they had rolled it about seventy-five feet downfield, the members of the team, still feeling other-worldly and unglued, plugged themselves in again.

The master of ceremonies spoke as dispassionately as he could into his pencil microphone. 'All departments at operational during this phase signify by beeping twice.'

Two tones rang across the canyon, startling the utter silence.

The booth technician asked, 'Is the audio analyzer ready? On a standby?'

The master of ceremonies, regaining some equilibrium now that he was doing something, said, 'If everything is ready here on the dark side of the moon, play the five tones.'

Shakespeare played the five notes very slowly.

There was no response from the phantom mass.

'*Encore*,' Lacombe ordered.

The five notes sounded through the night.

The great ship made a sound. It sounded like a pig grunting.

'Must have been something she ate,' the Team Leader said nervously.

The musician/engineer started playing the five notes again.

No response at all this time.

'Again,' the Team Leader said.

Shakespeare started playing.

Suddenly the last two notes were completed by the great mother ship. The noise was incredible. It blew the men back on their heels and shattered all the windows in all the cubicles. The booth technicians ducked the flying glass and some were cut, but too involved even to notice.

'Okay,' the Team Leader said, after a moment. 'Play it again.'

The synthesizer sounded and the ship responded. This time lights – matching the scoreboard's – flashed brilliantly across its surface.

Jillian Guiler knew she could not take any more of this alone. Frightened as she was, she felt it better to try to come down and find Neary. She needed to be with someone to help her survive all this. Jill picked up her little satchel and her Instamatic camera and started climbing down, following the path that Roy had taken.

The master of ceremonies said to Shakespeare and the booth technician, 'Give her six quavers, then pause.'

The musician played the notes.

The ship echoed these notes and then played a group of new notes that none of them had ever heard before.

The booth technician said, 'She gave us four quavers. A group of five quavers. A group of four semiquavers.'

Shakespeare imitated the ship's notes.

The ship added five new notes and five different colours.

Inside the computer cubicles, the technicians were in a sort of Nirvana. The ship was teaching them their musical and chromal vocabulary.

As the exchanges increased in complexity and speed, the computers took over from Shakespeare. He took his hands away from the keys and the Moog was played by the computers, like a player piano.

'Take everything from the lady,' the M.C. instructed the booth technician. 'Follow her pattern note for note.'

The mother ship exploded with sound and colour and the Moog, in interlock with the computer and the colour scoreboard, was playing right back. For several ecstatic minutes the great ship, the Moog and the scoreboard were actually jamming, like some sort of cosmic rock and light show.

It was very strange music – at one moment melodic and the next atonal, sometimes jazzy, then a little country-and-western, and the next moment something so grotesque and unmusical to their ears that they had to turn away.

Neary was smiling. He did not notice that Jill was now working her way through the crowd. Some of the technicians were clapping, some holding their heads. Lacombe had a dazed, glazed expression.

Suddenly, the ship stopped. It gave a few grunts, and then went silent. All its lights went out.

The base was deadly still and dark for a few moments.

And then the ship started opening.

The whole bottom end of it, beginning with a circumscribed sliver of surgical white light, opened into a furnace of light.

Everyone turned away. They put on their dark glasses and turned back. But even through their sunglasses it was hard to look directly into that burning light.

The thing opened more.

That was too much. Everyone moved back fast. They moved away from the unnerving light, which was now about one hundred and fifty yards wide.

The opening kept expanding.

First Lacombe, then Neary, and then the others stepped forward again. The white light gave off an intense heat, and then stopped.

Inside the bright heat they could see some movement.

The light was so bright that it sent rays out in all directions. Now there seemed to be eight different figures materializing out of the light. They seemed to be completely inhuman because the white light ate away their bodies into thin strips.

Then they were out of the ship and out of the light.

Lacombe walked toward them.

He – and the others – now saw that they were people. Men.

'I am Claude Lacombe,' the Frenchman said to the group.

The men appeared utterly dazed. They were dressed in 1940s naval air suits.

They were all very young and several of them were holding leather helmets and flight goggles in their hands.

They continued to walk forward numbly, in complete shock.

The first man stopped, half-saluted, and said, 'Frank Taylor. Lieutenant J.G. United States Navy Reserve. 064199.'

The M.C. stepped forward and shook his hand. 'Lieutenant, welcome home. This way to debriefing.

Two men led the lieutenant away.

5 Midnight's Children

Salman Rushdie

In the very centre of the sheet, a hole had been cut, a crude circle about seven inches in diameter.

'Close the door, ayah,' Ghani instructed the first of the lady wrestlers, and then, turning to Aziz, became confidential. 'This town contains many good-for-nothings who have on occasion tried to climb into my daughter's room. She needs,' he nodded at the three musclebound women, 'protectors.'

Aziz was still looking at the perforated sheet. Ghani said, 'All right, come on, you will examine my Naseem right now. *Pronto.*'

My grandfather peered around the room. 'But where is she, Ghani Sahib?' he blurted out finally. The lady wrestlers adopted supercilious expressions and, it seemed to him, tightened their musculatures, just in case he intended to try something fancy.

'Ah, I see your confusion,' Ghani said, his poisonous smile broadening, 'You Europe-returned chappies forget certain things. Doctor Sahib, my daughter is a decent girl, it goes without saying. She does not flaunt her body under the noses of strange men. You will understand that you cannot be permitted to see her, no, not in any circumstances; accordingly I have required her to be positioned behind that sheet. She stands there, like a good girl.'

A frantic note had crept into Doctor Aziz's voice. 'Ghani Sahib, tell me how I am to examine her without looking at her?' Ghani smiled.

'You will kindly specify which portion of my daughter it is necessary to inspect. I will then issue her with my instructions to place the required segment against that hole which you see there. And so, in this fashion the thing may be achieved.'

'But what, in any event, does the lady complain of?' – my grandfather, despairingly. To which Mr Ghani, his eyes rising upwards in their sockets, his smile twisting into a grimace of grief, replied: 'The poor child! She has a terrible, a too dreadful stomach ache.'

'In that case,' Doctor Aziz said with some restraint, 'will she show me her stomach, please.'

6 The Public Image
Muriel Spark

'You were wonderful,' Luigi said, fresh from watching, on the television, her entrance and exit from the hospital. He said, 'The orgy story is killed. Everyone knows now that Frederick was pursued to his death by women. There will be no orgy story at the inquest. I saw Billy O'Brien this afternoon. He gave me the name and address of Frederick's Marina.'

'Marina,' said Annabel, 'must be left out of it.'

'Why? We don't have to say at the inquest that she chased him in the church. That can be implied. You only need mention her name. Billy will have to testify, as being the last of his friends to see him alive. He'll confirm that Marina was one of the girls. Leave the rest to the newspapers.'

'She's out of it,' Annabel said. 'I've done a deal with her.'

She produced from the depth of her bag a bundle of letters which Luigi recognized as those suicide notes of Frederick's.

He said, 'You still have them – you haven't destroyed them – you take them around in your purse?'

'They're safest there. If I left them anywhere else they could be found. Tomorrow, when the banks open, I'll get Tom to put them in a safe deposit for me.'

Tom was her lawyer from London. He was to arrive very early next morning.

'You might lose your purse. It could be snatched.'

'I can't go out,' she said, looking at the window from where, in the morning, could be seen the café with the free young people sitting outside – 'Even in normal times I'm noticed and watched. No one could snatch my bag.'

'You should burn them,' Luigi said. 'Burn those letters and wash the ashes down the wash-basin. That's the way to do it.'

'I think I want to keep them. Anyway, Tom should see them. You've seen them, Billy's seen them, and my lawyer should see them. There might be talk afterwards, and if Tom has got to deny anything, it's better that he knows what he's denying.'

'Talk – what do you mean? Do you mean I'd talk of this?'

'Oh no,' she said very politely. 'I mean Billy, of course. After a thing like this has blown over, there's always the temptation to tell the inside story to one's friends. Five, ten years later, I mean.'

'You are very distrustful, Annabel. How can you think of five and ten years ahead when you're in difficulties already for tomorrow – the inquest, the chance – who knows? – that your public image will be ruined – we might have overlooked something – how can you count the years ahead like this?'

'How jumpy you are? A moment ago you were saying the inquest would be all right, and nothing to worry about.'

'Well, maybe, yes. Don't look too many years ahead. Actors can't do this.'

'I've got my baby for years ahead.'

'You should burn those letters and forget it. Billy was good not to have them photographed. He told me himself, and in fact I believe him, that the thought never crossed his mind. I asked him very many times, carefully, about that. I was ashamed afterwards, of asking these questions. It was good of Billy to bring them to you without making something for himself.'

'Good? What's good about not being bad?'

'You know the world. Billy is a good friend to you, Annabel. He has got Marina's address. He can mention her name in the courthouse. All the press will go to find her. She can't deny –'

'Wait, just wait a minute . . .' Annabel was taking one of the letters out of the bundle. She opened it. 'This is a new one,' she said.

She showed the letter to Luigi.

'Are you sure she had no copies made?'

'Oh yes. She probably doesn't know about photocopies. She only knows there's a story about Frederick being chased in the church, and she says it wasn't her. Neither it was. It was nobody.'

'Did you say you'd keep her name out of it if she gave you the letter?'

'Not really. She gave me the letter because she thought Frederick was mad. I was interested in that. If she thinks he was mad, then others would, too.'

'Not immediately.'

'With all those letters – so many? Even if what he's written about me were true, only a madman would go on about it so much to so many people. It's a case-history in itself, this bundle of letters.'

Luigi thought for a moment. Then he said, 'I agree that madness would be the only ultimate conclusion –'

'And one of the letters to his mother, who's dead,' Annabel said.

'Well, of course, that could be a symbolic letter. The Italian papers would certainly have loved that letter. All the more so if the mother's dead. We like letters to mothers, dead or alive.' He leaned forward, frowned, and said, quite harshly, 'The immediate reaction to those letters would have finished your movie career. You couldn't do any more of these films with me. There would have to be some other kind of movie for you, later on; and then you are getting older – middle, late thirties, and you will take a part, maybe, in something not so special. And I'd have to find another star, make a new start, right away, next week, with that.' He was pointing to her film script, which was now on top of a chest-of-drawers beside the window.

She said, 'I'm hungry.'

'Don't be tempted,' he said.

'I won't eat bread, potatoes or spaghetti,' she said. 'Don't worry, I won't get too fat for the part.'

He said in a milder voice, 'I meant, don't be tempted to show off those letters in the court-house.'

'Yes, I know that's what you meant. I want my dinner.'

'You should come out. Where would you like to go?'

'The nurse has left for the night. I don't want to leave the baby with anyone else.' She looked at her watch. 'Billy should be here soon,' she said. 'He can stay and have dinner with us up here, if you like, and we can get our story straight for tomorrow. There's only the doctor and Billy and me to give evidence.'

7 Indecent Exposure

Tom Sharpe

CHAPTER ONE

It was Heroes Day in Piemburg and as usual the little capital of Zululand was quite unwarrantably gay. Along the streets the jacarandas bloomed unconscionably beside gardens flamboyant with azaleas while from a hundred flagpoles Britons and Boers proclaimed their mutual enmity by flying the Union Jack or the Vierkleur, those emblems of the Boer War which neither side could ever forget. In separate ceremonies across the city the two white communities commemorated ancient victories. At the Anglican Cathedral the Bishop of Piemburg reminded his unusually large congregation that their ancestors had preserved freedom from such assorted enemies as Napoleon, President Kruger, the Kaiser and Adolf Hitler. At the Verwoerd Street Dutch Reformed Church the Reverend Schlachbals urged his flock never to forget that the British had invented concentration camps and that twenty-five thousand Boer women and children had been murdered in them. In short Heroes Day provided everyone with an opportunity to forget the present and revive old hatreds. Only the Zulus were forbidden to commemorate the occasion, partly on the grounds that they had no reputable heroes to honour but for the most part because it was felt that their participation would only lead to an increase in racial tension.

To Kommandant van Heerden, Piemburg's chief of police, the whole affair was most regrettable. As one of the few Afrikaners in Piemburg to be even slightly related to a hero (his grandfather had been shot by the British after the Battle of Paardeberg for ignoring the order to cease fire) he was expected to speak on the subject of heroism at the Nationalist rally at the Voortrekker Stadium and, besides, as one of the town's leading officials, he was obliged to attend the ceremony at Settlers Park where the Sons of England were inaugurating yet another wooden bench in honour of those who had fallen in the Zulu wars some hundred years before.

In the past the Kommandant had been able to avoid all these engagements by pleading the impossibility of being in two places at the same time but since the police had recently been allocated a helicopter, this year he was denied that excuse. At intervals throughout the day the helicopter could be seen chattering across the city while the Kommandant, who disliked heights almost as much as he did public speaking, sorted through his notes in an effort to find something to say whenever he landed. Since his notes were ones he had used annually since the Congo Crisis years before, their illegibility and general lack of relevance caused some confusion. At the Voortrekker Stadium Kommandant van Heerden's speech on heroism included the assurance that the citizens of Piemburg need have no doubt that the South African Police would leave no stone unturned to see that nothing disturbed the even tenor of their lives, while at Settlers Park his eloquence on behalf of the nuns who had been raped in the Congo, coming as it did after a passionate plea for racial harmony by a Methodist missionary, was considered not to be in the best of taste.

Finally, to round the day's business off, there was a parade of his men at the Mounted Police Barracks at which the Mayor had agreed to award a trophy for conspicuous bravery and devotion to duty.

'Interesting what you had to say about those nuns,' said the Mayor as the helicopter lifted off the ground at Settlers Park, 'I'd almost forgotten about them. Must be twelve years ago that happened.'

'I think it's just as well to remind ourselves that it could happen here,' said the Kommandant.

'I suppose so. Funny thing the way kaffirs always seem to go for nuns. You'd think they'd like something a bit more jolly.'

'It's probably because they're virgins,' said the Kommandant.

'How very clever of you to think of that,' said the Mayor, 'my wife will be relieved to hear it.'

Below them the roofs glowed in the afternoon sun. Built in the heyday of the British Empire, the tiny metropolis still possessed an air of seedy grandeur. The City Hall, redbrick Gothic, loomed above the market square while, opposite, the Supreme Court maintained a classic formal air. Behind the railway station, Fort Rapier, once the headquarters of the British Army and now a mental hospital, stood outwardly unaltered. Patients shuffled across the great parade ground where once ten thousand men had marched and wheeled before departing for the front. The Governor's Palace had been turned into a teacher training college and students sunbathed on lawns which had once been the scene of garden parties and receptions. To Kommandant van Heerden it was all very puzzling and sad and he was just wondering why the British had abandoned their Empire so easily when the helicopter steadied itself over the Police Barracks and began to descend.

'A very fine turn-out,' said the Mayor indicating the ranks of police konstabels on the parade ground below.

'I suppose so,' said the Kommandant, recalled from past splendours to the drab present. He looked down at the five hundred men drawn up in front of a saluting base. There was certainly nothing splendid about them, nor about the six Saracen armoured cars parked in a line behind them. As the helicopter bumped to the ground and its blades finally stopped turning, he helped the

Mayor down and escorted him to the platform. The police band broke into a rousing march while sixty-nine guard dogs snarled and slobbered in several iron cages vacated for the occasion by the black prisoners who were normally confined in them while awaiting trail.

'After you,' said the Kommandant at the foot of the steps that led to the platform. At the top a tall thin luitenant was standing, holding the leash of a particularly large Dobermann Pinscher, whose teeth, the Mayor noted with alarm, were bared in what appeared to be an immutable snarl.

'No, after you,' said the Mayor.

'I insist. After you,' said the Kommandant.

'Listen,' said the Mayor, 'if you think I'm going to dispute these steps with that Dobermann . . .'

Kommandant van Heerden smiled.

'Nothing to worry about,' he said. 'It's stuffed. That's the trophy.' He lurched on to the platform and pushed the Dobermann aside with his knee. The Mayor followed him up and was introduced to the thin luitenant.

'Luitenant Verkramp, head of the Security Branch,' said the Kommandant.

Luitenant Verkramp smiled bleakly and the Major sat down in the knowledge that he had just met a representative of BOSS, the Bureau of State Security whose reputation for torturing suspects was second to none.

'I'll just make a short speech,' said the Kommandant, 'and then you can award the trophy.' The Mayor nodded and the Kommandant went to the microphone.

'Mr Mayor, ladies and gentlemen, officers of the South African Police,' he shouted, 'we are gathered here today to pay tribute to the heroes of South African history and in particular to honour the memory of the late Konstabel Els whose recent tragic death has deprived Piemburg of one of its most outstanding policemen.'

The Kommandant's voice amplified by the loudspeaker system boomed across the parade ground and lost in the process all trace of the hesitancy he felt in mentioning the name Els. It had been Luitenant Verkramp's idea to award the stuffed Dobermann as a trophy and, glad to see the thing moved from his office, the Kommandant had agreed. Now faced with the prospect of eulogizing the dead Els, he wasn't so sure it had been a wise decision. In life Els had shot more blacks dead in the course of duty than any other policeman in South Africa and had been a constant offender against the Immorality Laws. The Kommandant looked down at his notes and ploughed on.

'A loyal comrade, a fine citizen, a devout Christian . . .' To the Mayor, looking down at the faces of the konstabels before him, it was clear that Konstabel Els' death had indeed been a great loss to the Piemburg constabulary. Certainly none of the faces he could see suggested those admirable characteristics which had evidently been so manifest in Konstabel Els. He was just coming to the conclusion that the average IQ must be in the region of 65 when the Kommandant finished his speech and announced that the Els

Memorial Trophy had been won by Konstabel van Rooyen. The Mayor stood up and took the leash of the stuffed Dobermann from Luitenant Verkramp.

'Congratulations on winning this award,' he said when the prizewinner presented himself. 'And what did you do to be so highly honoured?'

Konstabel van Rooyen blushed and mumbled something about shooting a kaffir.

'He prevented a prisoner from escaping,' the Kommandant explained hurriedly.

'Very commendable, I'm sure,' said the Mayor and handed the leash to the konstabel. To the cheers of his fellow policemen and the applause of the public the winner of the Els Memorial Trophy staggered down the steps carrying the stuffed Dobermann as the band struck up.

'Splendid idea giving a trophy like that,' the Mayor said as they sipped tea in the refreshment tent afterwards, 'though I must say I would never have thought of a stuffed dog. Highly original.'

'It was killed by the late Konstabel Els himself,' the Kommandant said.

'He must have been a remarkable man.'

'With his bare hands,' said the Kommandant.

'Dear God,' said the Mayor.

Presently, leaving the Mayor discussing the advisability of allowing visiting Japanese businessmen to use Whites Only swimming pools with the Rev Schlachbals, the Kommandant moved away. At the entrance of the tent Luitenant Verkramp was deep in conversation with a large blonde whose turquoise dress fitted her astonishingly well. Under the pink picture hat the Kommandant recognized the features of Dr von Blimenstein, the eminent psychiatrist at Fort Rapier Mental Hospital.

'Getting free treatment?' the Kommandant asked jocularly as he edged past.

'Dr von Blimenstein has been telling me how she deals with cases of manic-depression,' said the Luitenant.

Dr von Blimenstein smiled. 'Luitenant Verkramp seems most interested in the use of electro-convulsive therapy.'

'I know,' said the Kommandant and wandered out into the open air, idly speculating on the possibility that Verkramp was attracted to the blonde psychiatrist. It seemed unlikely somehow but with Luitenant Verkramp one never knew.

8 The World According to Garp

John Irving

So Garp sat squirming in School of Nursing Hall. He twisted the itchy rope braids of his ridiculous purse, a scraggily hemp thing with an oriental design, barely big enough to hold his wallet. In her large, bursting shoulder bag, Roberta Muldoon had hidden Garp's real clothes – his other identity.

'This is Manda Horton-Jones,' Roberta whispered, indicating a thin, hawk-nosed woman speaking nasally and with her rodential head pointed down; she read a stiff, prepared speech.

Garp didn't know who Manda Horton-Jones was; he shrugged, enduring her. The speeches had ranged from strident, political calls for unity to disturbed, painful personal reminiscenses of Jenny Fields. The audience did not know whether to applaud or to pray – whether to voice approval or to nod grimly. The atmosphere was both one of mourning and one of urgent togetherness – with a strong sense of marching forth. Thinking about it, Garp supposed this was natural and fitting, both to his mother and to his dim perception of what the women's movement *was*.

'This is Sally Devlin,' Roberta whispered. The woman now climbing to the speakers' platform looked pleasant and wise and vaguely familiar. Garp felt immediately the need to defend himself from her. He didn't mean it, but solely to goad Roberta, Garp whispered, 'She has nice legs.'

'Nicer than yours,' Roberta said, pinching his thigh painfully between her strong thumb and her long, pass-catching index finger – one of the fingers, Garp supposed, that had been broken so many times during Roberta's fling as a Philadelphia Eagle.

Sally Devlin looked down on them with her soft, sad eyes as if she were silently scolding a classroom of children who were not paying attention – not even sitting still.

'That senseless murder does not really merit all this,' she said, quietly. 'But Jenny Fields simply helped so many *individuals*, she simply was so patient and generous with women who were having a bad time. Anyone who's ever been helped by someone else should feel terrible about what's happened to her.'

Garp felt truly terrible, at that moment; he heard a combined sigh and sob of hundreds of women. Beside him, Roberta's broad shoulders shook against him. He felt a hand, perhaps of the woman sitting directly behind him, grip his own shoulder, cramped in the terrible turquoise jump suit. He wondered if he was about to be slapped for his offensive, inappropriate attire, but the hand just held on to his shoulder. Perhaps the woman needed support. At this moment, Garp knew, they all felt like sisters, didn't they?

He looked up to see what Sally Devlin was saying, but his own eyes were teary and he could not see Ms Devlin clearly. He could *hear* her, though: she was sobbing. Great heartfelt and heaving cries! She was trying to get back to her speech but her eyes couldn't find her place on the page; the page rattled against the microphone. Some very powerful-looking woman, whom Garp thought he had seen before – one of those bodyguard types he had often seen with his mother – tried to help Sally Devlin off the platform, but Ms Devlin didn't want to leave.

'I wasn't going to do this,' she said, still crying – meaning her sobs, her loss of control. 'I had more to say,' she protested, but she could not get hold of her voice. 'Damn it,' she said, with a dignity that moved Garp.

The big tough-looking woman found herself alone at the microphone. The audience waited quietly. Garp felt a tremble, or maybe a tug, from the hand on his shoulder. Looking at Roberta's large hands, folded in her lap, Garp knew that the hand on his shoulder must be very small.

The big tough-looking woman wanted to say something, and the audience waited. But they would wait forever to hear a word from her. Roberta knew her. Roberta stood up beside Garp and began to applaud the big, hard-looking woman's silence – her exasperating quiet in front of the microphone. Other people joined Roberta's applause – even Garp, though he had no idea why he was clapping.

'She's an Ellen Jamesian,' Roberta whispered to him. 'She *can't* say anything.' Yet the woman melted the audience with her pained, sorry face. She opened her mouth as if she were singing, but no sound came out. Garp imagined he could see the severed stump of her tongue. He remembered how his mother supported them – these crazies; Jenny was wonderful to every single one of them who came to her. But Jenny had finally admitted her disapproval of what they had done – perhaps only to Garp. 'They're making victims of themselves,' Jenny had said, 'and yet that's the same thing they're angry at men for doing to them. Why don't they just take a vow of silence, or never speak in a man's presence?' Jenny said. 'It's not logical: to maim yourself to make a point.'

But Garp, now touched by the mad woman in front of him, felt the whole history of the world's self-mutilation – though violent and illogical, it expressed, perhaps like nothing else, a terrible hurt. 'I am really *hurt*,' said the woman's huge face, dissolving before him in his own swimmy tears.

Then the little hand on his shoulder hurt *him*; he remembered himself – a man at a ritual for women – and he turned around to see the rather tired-looking young woman behind him. Her face was familiar, but he didn't recognize her.

'I know you,' the young woman whispered to him. She did not sound *happy* that she knew him, either.

Roberta had warned him not to open his mouth to anyone, not even to *try* to speak. He was prepared for handling that problem. He shook his head. He took a pad of paper out of the flap pocket, which was crushed against his mammoth, false bosom, and he snatched a pencil out of his absurd purse. The sharp, clawlike fingers of the woman bit into his shoulder, as if she were keeping him from running away.

Hi! I'm an Ellen Jamesian,

Garp scribbled on the pad; he tore the slip off and handed it to the young woman. She didn't take it.

'Like hell you are,' she said. 'You're T. S. Garp.'

The word *Garp* bounced like the burp of an unknown animal into the silence of the suffering auditorium, still conducted by the quiet Ellen Jamesian on stage. Roberta Muldoon turned around and looked panic-stricken; she had never seen this particular young lady in her life.

9 Telephone Conversation
Wole Soyinka

The price seemed reasonable, location
Indifferent. The landlady swore she lived
Off premises. Nothing remained
But self-confession. 'Madam,' I warned,
'I hate a wasted journey – I am African.'
Silence. Silenced transmission of
Pressurized good-breeding. Voice, when it came,
Lipstick coated, long gold-rolled
Cigarette-holder pipped. Caught I was, foully.
'HOW DARK?' . . . I had not misheard . . .'ARE YOU LIGHT
OR VERY DARK?' Button B. Button A. Stench
Of rancid breath of public hide-and-speak.
Red booth. Red pillar-box. Red double-tiered
Omnibus squelching tar. It *was* real! Shamed
By ill-mannered silence, surrender
Pushed dumbfoundment to beg simplification.
Considerate she was, varying the emphasis –
'ARE YOU DARK? OR VERY LIGHT?' Revelation came.
'You mean – like plain or milk chocolate?'
Her assent was clinical, crushing in its light
Impersonality. Rapidly, wave-length adjusted,
I chose. 'West African sepia' – and as afterthought,
'Down in my passport.' Silence for spectroscopic
Flight of fancy, till truthfulness clanged her accent
Hard on the mouthpiece. 'WHAT'S THAT?' conceding
'DON'T KNOW WHAT THAT IS.' 'Like brunette.'
'THAT'S DARK, ISN'T IT?' 'Not altogether.
Facially, I am brunette, but madam, you should see
The rest of me. Palm of my hand, soles of my feet
Are a peroxide blonde. Friction, caused –
Foolishly madam – by sitting down, has turned

My bottom raven black – One moment madam!' – sensing
Her receiver rearing on the thunderclap
About my ears – 'Madam,' I pleaded, 'wouldn't you rather
See for yourself?'

Sport

1 The Greatest – My Own Story

Muhammad Ali with Richard Durham

Extract A

CHAPTER ONE

SHORTY IS WATCHING

Louisville 100 miles. I barely see the sign in the rain.

'Won't make it by morning,' Harold Hazzard, my driver, says. He has been at the wheel too long and is driving with just the edge of his mind.

'We will if I drive.' I know every bend and curve in the road from here. When I take the wheel, Harold joins the rest of my camp crew in the back of the bus. Belinda and my daugher Maryum are back there too, fast asleep.

'Worst place in the world is an old hometown when you're down,' Chris Dundee once warned me. 'Let them remember you as a winner; never come home beaten.'

Until now, I had always come home like the victorious hunter bringing back big game from the jungle: two Golden Gloves Championships, some AAU titles, an Olympic Gold Medal, the World Heavyweight Title. Even exiled and barred from boxing, I came back as The Undefeated.

Now it's the spring of 1973 and I'm coming home after a defeat every man, woman and child in my hometown saw or heard about, just like everybody else all over the world. The press will crowd the sports pages with headlines that remind me: MUHAMMAD IS FINISHED! END OF AN ERA! ALI BEATEN BY A NOBODY! BIG MOUTH SHUT FOR ALL TIME! MOST THRILLING FIGHT IN HISTORY!

I want to come home. To rest. To see Bird and my father and old friends. To see where I am. To remember who I am, where I came from and where I want to go. I was born, bred and spent the first twenty-one years of my life there. I have to know if it's really 'home' – the place you can go to when you're whipped.

The rain pours down heavier and I slow up to see the road better. Squinting out into the darkness, mile after mile, I keep going over the same scene, like in a movie: San Diego Sports Arena. The last round is over. I'm standing in my corner. The referee is collecting the judges' votes. He looks at them, calls off the scoring, glances my way for a second, then turns to Norton. 'The winner by a split decision – Ken Norton!'

The stadium explodes. Wild shouts and screams come down from the bleachers. Some boo the decision, but the screams and cries of 'NORTON!' 'NORTON!' drown them out.

'We beat you, you bastard!' I look down at a heavyset white man who has jumped up on his chair yelling up at me, waving a newspaper. 'We got you! We got you!'

Policemen leap into the ring, but people break past them, pouring in under the ropes. Joe Frazier is hugging Norton, who is his stablemate and sparring partner. A radio commentator is yelling for me to come over, 'say something to explain it'. But Angelo and Bundini are already moving me down the steps. I taste blood draining into my throat and the pain in my face and shoulders is growing. I remember pausing and looking over to where I know Belinda is sitting. I want to wave at her, give her some sign that I'm all right, but the police and the crowd are shoving against each other and I'm pushed toward the dressing room.

'Who's the prettiest *now*?' . . . 'Who's the prettiest *now*?' A cluster of white women are shouting at the top of their voices and stomping their feet. The police move them aside.

My head feels as though it will drop off. The pain in the left side of my jaw is almost more than I can stand.

A man in a fireman's uniform breaks through the police line: 'You finished, loud-mouth! You finished!'

The police form a wedge in front of me, forcing the crowd back until we get out of the arena and down the hall. The hecklers follow, screaming, chanting, booing while the ushers try to open the dressing-room door. Finally it opens from the inside and one by one we squeeze through – Herbert Muhammad, my manager; Bundini, my assistant trainer; Dr Pacheco, my ringside doctor; Captain Joseph Yuseff of Temple No. 7, who I've known since the first day I joined the Nation of Islam; Angelo Dundee, my trainer; Lloyd Wells, an old friend; Eugene Kilroy and Hassan Salami, my aides; Howard Bingham, my photographer; Dick Durham, my writer; Reggie Barrett, another friend; Pat Patterson, security guard; Walter Youngblood, assistant trainer . . . Even after we're in, they keep pushing the door open to make sure I can hear them: 'Who's the greatest *now*?'

At last the door is closed and Angelo is leaning against it, exhausted. He can't believe the hatred and fury in those voices. 'Savages!' is all he can say.

Kilroy is picking up the robe that dropped from my shoulders, THE PEOPLE'S CHAMPION across the back of it – a gift from Elvis Presley, who had it made when I fought Joe Bugner. He comes over and wraps a towel under my chin and over my head to ease the strain on my jaw.

'This is Norton's town. Norton's people,' someone is saying. 'Like Louisville is your town, Ali. Just a hometown reaction to a local boy.'

But I know those faces, those voices out there are not just a 'hometown reaction'. It's the reaction of most of White America. I'm used to having half the audience come to see me get beat, regardless of who my opponent is. I've denied them this day for a long time, and now that it's here, they're making the most of it. They haven't had much to cheer about since Frazier dropped me with a left hook in Madison Square Garden. And this defeat is much sweeter to them because I'm beaten not by Frazier or Foreman, internationally qualified monsters, but by a 'local boy'.

Extract B

The crowd eggs me on: 'ALI! ALI! BOMAYE!'

I hear Kid Gavilan, the old Cuban Champion of a thousand fights, telling me, 'Ali, the crowd'll push you on like they own a piece of you, like there's something in their life that depends on whether you live or die. And you'll get into something too deep to back down. You've been calling out, "I'm the prettiest. I'm the greatest. See how pretty I am. Not a scratch!" They laugh, but one day the people will test you out. They will send you into a den to take meat out of the lion's mouth and see who comes out the prettiest. If you die trying, they'll be sorry for you, but if you back down they'll remember you as a phony forever. When you fight for the title, you lay it all on the line.'

I know it's time for the test. I see George trying to lumber back, to regain his poise. I shoot a straight right to his jaw with all the snap and power that's in me. I strike him almost flush on the chin, and he stands still.

Archie Moore will say the blow would have knocked out anybody but I know, had I thrown it in the earlier rounds, George would have been strong enough to shake it off.

I'm ready to follow through with combinations, but I see he's slowly falling, a dazed look in his eyes. I know he's entering the room of the half-dream for the first time in his life. George is down, his eyes glazed. He's listening to the tuning forks humming in his head, bats blowing saxophones, alligators whistling, neon signs blinking.

The referee begins the count. George will later protest that he was the victim of a short count, and I can understand why. In the half-dream room time seems to stretch out slow, like rubber, and unless you've been there before, you'll never know how fast it goes by.

I watch every lift of the referee's arm. I remember thinking again of Frazier. He would never lose the crown lying on the floor. No referee could count over his body as long as he had blood in it.

'Six . . . seven . . . eight . . .'

George is turning over slowly.

'Nine . . . ten!'

George is on his feet, but it's over. The referee raises my hand in victory.

And the stadium explodes. People break past the paratroopers and climb over the press tables, climb into the ring.

Archie has wrapped his arms around George, and I holler, 'Archie, am I too old?'

Archie jerks his head my way. There's a gleam in his eye. He raises his fists and shouts, 'Your time is coming! Your day will come!'

And this I know. But the referee is raising *my* hand, and the whole world is screaming, 'ALI! ALI! ALI! ALI!'

A reporter claws his way through the crowd and yells at me, 'How did you do it, World Heavyweight Champion! What you think of George now?'

I shake my head. I want to go to my dressing room. I don't want to tell him what George has taught me. That too many victories weaken you. That the defeated can rise up stronger than the victor.

But I take nothing away from George. He can still beat any man in the world.

Except me.

2 Journey to Wembley

Brian James

Extract A

A Cup Final is a drama and it has a script. Losers, too, have lines to follow. They shake hands with the winners, smile wanly over their medals, wave to their crowd and walk away to leave the stage for those rejoicing. And there at the entrance of the tunnel, leaving sunshine that bears down like a spotlight, cold reality returns. Clemence is first. He is a big, generally gentle, man . . . he would trample down children as he covers the next 50 yards, staring sightlessly ahead.

Then Keegan. Trotting. A TV hand grabs him around the shoulders and steers him towards a waiting interviewer-and-camera; he goes without protest, as though to an execution with no hope of reprieve. Kennedy managers a wide grin and a joke for photographers. The grin drops from his face like a shutter two paces further on. Then Case, head down and muttering. Then Jones, head up, eyes misty.

Smith follows, blazing with anger. He has a fistful of the injured Phil Thompson's 'civvie clothing'. He is demonstrating the winning goal. 'He'd got my (effing) shirt. Like this. Pulling me out of it! Greenhoff! And that effing ref stood there. . . .' His voice fades off down the tunnel.

Hughes is last. He sees you. Knows you, and an innate courtesy makes him pause. But his mind is in neutral. And he tries to say something, and can't. Tries to smile, and doesn't quite manage that either. So he punches you in the side and moves on. Wiping his eyes on a scarf thrown by a fan.

Inside the Liverpool dressing-room there is a silence that screams. Players move about like men under water. Some begin stripping for the bath. Most just sit. It doesn't seem possible that you can have 20 men gazing around a medium-sized room and none of them meeting another eye. Yet they manage it.

Since we began this journey we have seen a few losers' dressing-rooms. That was inevitable, part of the shape of the assignment. You start to tell yourself that they were *all* like this – the same bits of bandage about the floor, the same litter of soiled shirts that had seemed such brave uniforms two hours before. But there is a difference. Not because the royal-blue carpet makes this a posher place than Tividale, but because of the scale of what has been lost.

Other sides have lost a game, a chance, a bonus. Liverpool have lost their place in history. One day some side may do the treble. Maybe even a side from

Liverpool's single reply came between the two United goals when Jimmy Case brought down a cross, swivelled on it and volleyed into the top corner of the net. Stepney never had a chance.

Liverpool. But not these men. The disappointment is so intense that hardly anyone – even the press the following day – mentions that Liverpool have also just failed to become the fifth club in history to win the Double.

The door opens to admit the FA Secretary Ted Croker. He is flustered and apologetic. There's been a mix-up. The Duchess has given two of Manchester's winner's medals to Liverpool losers: Hughes and Heighway indifferently reach up and hand over their blue boxes . . . get red ones in return. Normally such an incident would have brought a tirade of mickey-taking: Mr. Croker escapes in silence . . . it's still too early for sarcasm.

Ray Kennedy sighs theatrically, 'One day, perhaps we'll even win a match.' No-one smiles. It is still too early for laughs. Bob Paisley starts to talk: 'Well that one's over, but we have still got the big 'un coming on Wednesday. . . .' His voice, too, tails off. It's too early for lectures.

More of that appalling silence. What *are* they thinking? Keegan stares across the room . . . looking into the past hour? Or his future? Then you sense what it is at the core of this mood – self-accusation. All of them have done what they could; but a few have not done what they were capable of. It is this discrepancy that now haunts them.

Terry McDermott suddenly grabs a Muppet: it's Kermit, the green frog. 'What a bloody mascot you turned out. Rubbish, you.' He holds it a minute then boots it explosively across the room. It lies for a while under a bench, being glared at. Then coach Ronnie Moran picks it up, brushes it down and places it in a kit hamper; he knows things said and done now will be regretted later.

Clemence leaps to his feet. 'I know what's got to be done,' he claims. 'Only one thing for it . . . tonight I am going to get SOOOOOOO pissed.' Many funnier things have been said in football. But for some reason this is the ice-breaker . . . gales of laughter. The dressing-room takes a breath, and begins to return to life.

The staff all start talking at once. Paisley, and his coaches Moran and Fagan: 'You were not disgraced' . . . 'Just wasn't our day' . . . 'Got to get our heads up for the *real* one' . . . 'Played worse a dozen times and won.' All the usual clichés. They don't address their remarks to anyone in particular . . . just spray the room, as though their words are disinfectant to destroy any germs of doubt. The players' banter also begins. Clemence and Smith start nagging scout Ben Bennett about Manchester's second goal . . . 'Seen 'em a dozen times, you have, never mentioned they go for in-off shots did you? That wasn't on the dossier . . . you . . . you're *useless*.'

Hughes claims he's had news about the team's record 'We Can Do It'. 'It's still No. 1 in the charts. In Peru. But it's dropped to 87 here. How about a follow-up disc . . . "We Can Nearly Do It"?'

Keegan insists he has just discovered some consolation: 'It's still better coming here with Liverpool than with England. That's the first time in two years I've got off that pitch without the crowd singing "What a load of rubbish".'

The players, dressed now, leave to find their womenfolk. Going out they hear the gusts of hysterical laughter from United's dressing-room – just 10 paces across the corridor, but light years away in mood. No-one begrudges United that . . . they paid their deposit on this pleasure with last year's pain.

I walk around the empty track with Hughes. You can't walk in silence, so you start to speak. 'Emlyn, look . . . I know . . .' and fall quiet. 'Yeah,' he says. 'There are no words, are there? But thanks anyway.'

We go a little way and he begins again: 'I've been here a few times. Great place to win. But it guts the losers. I feel for the lads like Jimmy Case – Christ, what a game *he* had – and Joey Jones and Terry McDermott. That Terry, only young and *twice* he's lost. You feel it most for them. No, that's not right. You feel it most for yourself. Losing here . . . no-one will ever get hardened to that.'

Extract B

Below stairs, Bob Paisley, collar and tie askew and sweating buckets, came up to meet the world's Press. He looked as bewildered as a man who had stood for election as Peoples' Warden and found when the votes were counted he had become Prime Minister. Yet, though blinded by TV lights, bedevilled by a translation device that bombarded him with his own words in French, German and Italian, he carried it off with a politician's ease.

Then back to the hotel for the party. It would probably be easier to detail every shot of a civil war than to convey a complete picture of this celebration; I can only give glimpses. Like seeing a fan creep into the banqueting room, run to the table to kiss the Cup, and back reverently out, or another supporter who sought out every player in turn and knelt before him, explaining 'Dey's royalty . . . dat's why' . . . or a third Kopite of ferocious mien and stupendously drunk, swaying in front of Minister of Sport Denis Howell: 'We are going to have the greatest booze-up ever . . . but don't worry Mister, we ain't Leeds . . . and we ain't Manchester United . . . we'll behave. Dat's a promise.' (A promise absolutely kept – Italian papers next day praised Liverpool's football *and* lavishly apologised for the harsh things they'd predicted about the supporters.)

At first the fans were kept outside. But Emlyn Hughes (who managed the feat of ending the year as a footballer of fabulous achievement and still a very nice man) kept spotting faces above the policeman's helmets – and making a dash for the door with a fresh bottle of champagne. Eventually, though, the cordon broke . . . the mob burst in, took turns at being pictured with the players, or swigging from the cup. At one time the huge trophy vanished: 'Never fret,' said a Liverpool official, 'it's outside being trooped around the grounds by the fans. Scared? Listen, if we forget it, it'll turn up at Anfield in two days . . . unmarked and polished like new.'

The party splintered up and was carted to various bedrooms. And around the pool, where Phil Neal got ducked and Keegan got a black eye, and those of us still with a bit to do tried to find a quiet corner to talk and make a few notes, Hughes told me, 'Did I think we'd do it. You want the truth? No. Not after Saturday. I put on the bravest face I could. But deep down I thought we'd left it all behind at Wembley. But once we started to play . . . I knew nothing could stop us. Now . . . I didn't know it was possible for any man to feel this happy. Only one doubt . . . what the hell do we do for an encore? The treble? No way . . . we are the team of the century . . . and no side will ever get nearer. It can't be done.'

Tommy Smith had this to say: 'I told my missus I'd finish for Liverpool by scoring in the Cup. We both thought I meant at Wembley. But soon as Steve pinged that corner at me I knew this was it. Their keeper is a giant . . . but he looked like a mouse on the line when I headed at him. Even so the ball took 10 minutes to hit the net. Who'd have thought me, Tommy Smith'd end up with a Roy of the Rovers stunt like that? Now . . . I'm going to get a gold plate put in me nut . . . to mark the spot. After this, there'll be such a crowd at my testimonial on Friday, I can afford it.'

Next morning around dawn, weary waiters cleared away 385 empty champagne bottles, and tireless players tossed passing reporters into the pool and gardeners prodded bushes and Liverpool fans fell blinking into the sunlight, and every hill in view from the roof of the hotel had little knots of red figures lurching around asking each other, 'What happened to the last coach back to Kirkby?' and it was all over.

Well, not quite. Liverpool still had to fly home – using up 100 more bottles of champagne to cure the collective hangover – and then suffer the ordeal of a 10-mile drive in from Speke with 500,000 out in the streets, 20-deep in places, and listen to speeches, and wave until their arms were leaden and grin until their jaws locked, and wonder with Steve Heighway 'What now? Honestly I almost envy Kevin leaving; how the hell are we going to find motivation next season after this?'

Liverpool lasted in the headlines a few days more: Keegan went to complete his £500,000 transfer to Hamburg; Smith was persuaded *not* to retire after a testimonial that drew 37,000 to Anfield and so signed a new two-year contract; and Joey Jones refused the offer of a rest and dashed down to Wrexham to play for Wales.

There was even another Cup to go for . . . the World Club Championship which could pit Liverpool against the best side in South America. Bob Paisley said, 'No thanks! Not after what happened to Manchester United and Celtic . . . nothing but riots and all that. We know where we stand . . . we'll leave titles like "The World's Greatest" to Muhammed Ali!'

3 Looks and Smiles

Barry Hines

She began to dread United coming over the halfway line and became a secret Chelsea supporter, willing them to keep the ball at the other end. The crowd across there kept falling forward too, and the waves of movement down the Kop were like shadows racing down a hill. Watching these surges made Karen feel worse, especially when a body was lifted above the heads of the crowd and passed down to waiting ambulance men at the front.

'Mick?'

The United goalkeeper rolled the ball to a full-back on the edge of the penalty area.

'Mick!'

'What?'

'I feel sick.'

The full-back passed to a mid-field player who had moved into a space on the wing.

'What did you say?'

'I said I feel sick. I don't feel well.'

The mid-field player began to dribble the ball up the touch line.

'You'll be all right.'

'I think I'm going to be sick. It must be that hot dog I had outside.'

'It'll go off.'

The mid-field man was allowed to run twenty yards with the ball before he was challenged.

'I feel awful. All hot and dizzy.'

The United player tried to beat an opponent, but the ball bounced out of play off the other man's legs. This gave Mick the chance to have a quick look at Karen before the ball-boy threw it back. Her pallor was obvious even through her make-up, and there was sweat on her top lip.

'You're not going to faint, are you?'

'I don't know what I'm going to do. I just feel awful.'

The throw-in was taken and United continued their attack.

'That's all I need, you fainting and me walking round the side of the pitch with the stretcher. I'd never live it down. The lads'd crucify me.'

Karen touched her forehead, then looked to see if her fingertips were damp.

'Never mind the lads. What about me?'

'What do you want to do, then?'

'I'll have to go out.'

Mick turned and looked at her even though the ball was still in play.

'You what? We can't do that!'

'I'll have to, Mick, I feel terrible.'

She leaned against him and rested her head on his shoulder. Chelsea regained the ball near the halfway line and began an attack of their own. Karen closed her eyes. She was getting heavier on his arm. Mick stood her upright and turned round.

'Come on, then. But I'm coming straight back in, I can tell you.'

And he began to force his way back up the terracing holding her hand. Most of the people that they squeezed past hardly saw or felt them this time, they were too intent on the game. But the man who had queried Mick's manners on the way down did. And if Mick had looked angry then, he looked demented now. The man kept quiet and shouted to United to 'Come on!'

They reached the top of the terrace and began to walk down the deserted steps at the other side. Karen held the hand rail and Mick held her arm at the other side. From this height, they could see the traffic on the main road outside the Ground and the roofs of terraced houses slotting into each other as they stretched away towards the steelworks in the distance.

Mick kicked an empty Fanta orange drink can down the steps, then kicked it again when he met it further down.

'It's the last time I'm bringing you, I can tell you.'

'I can't help it, can I? I'm not doing it on purpose.'

When they reached the bottom, Karen sat down on the steps and covered her face with her hands. Mick stood by impatiently, looking from Karen to the backs of the spectators framed in the entrance at the top of the steps. Their gestures reflected the fortunes of the game and after one particularly loud shout, and what turned out to be a premature raising of the arms to celebrate a goal, Mick became increasingly agitated.

'Do you feel any better now?'

Karen shook her head without raising it from her hands.

'I feel awful.'

'What do you want to do then?'

'I want to go home.'

'Go home! They've only just kicked off! You're going on your own if you do, I'm telling you now.'

He noticed the Fanta can again and kicked it against a lavatory wall. It stopped where it fell. It was the wrong shape to roll anywhere now.

'Stop shouting will you? You're making me feel worse.'

Mick relented slightly when she started to cry, and he was just about to sit down and put his arm around her, when there was an outburst from inside the Ground that could only mean one thing.

Mick spun round and looked up. At the top of the steps people were jumping up and down waving scarves and hugging each other. From the bottom of the steps, where the reason for their behaviour was not apparent, they looked as if they had gone mad.

'They've scored!'

Mick dashed up the steps to join them and was immediately absorbed into the celebrations as he pushed forward to see what was happening on the pitch. He reappeared seconds later and ran down the steps again just as fast. He was panting when he reached the bottom. Karen was still sitting on the steps facing the boundary wall, along the top of which shards of glass glinted in the pale afternoon sunlight. After one miserable performance by United, Mick had heard a supporter remark that the glass had been put there to stop people getting *out* of the Ground.

'Come on then, make your mind up. What are you going to do?'

Karen stood up. She was still crying. The damp tissue in her hand had changed from pink to crimson.

'I'm going home.'

'Hurry up, then. That's one goal I've missed. They'll get a bagful against this lot.'

They walked across to a turnstile and the man inside counting the takings let them through. He watched them curiously as the gate clunked round. United had just scored; he was wearing a red scarf; she was crying . . . Mick read his thoughts; and with a nod towards Karen followed by a glance towards the heavens, tried to explain the strangeness of the circumstances.

'Don't lock up, will you? I'm coming back in.'

Mick stopped on the pavement just outside the turnstile to make sure.

'You know where the bus stop is, don't you?'

Karen shook her head. She did not look at him.

'It's at the end of the street, just across the road. You'll see it. You want the 84.'

She walked away immediately. She seemed determined not to say any more, but as she drew level with a poster on the wall advertising the next home fixture she turned round.

'I've finished with you, Mick Walsh. You're horrible! I never want to see you again!'

Mick was astounded! Horrible! How could he be? He had deserted his mates to bring her. Risked being ridiculed if he had been seen. Bought her a hot dog.

4 Professional Foul

Tom Stoppard

10. INT. ANDERSON'S ROOM. NIGHT

ANDERSON *is lying fully dressed on the bed. His eyes open. Only light from the window. There are faint voices from* GRAYSON'*s room. After a while* ANDERSON *gets up and leaves his room and knocks on* GRAYSON'*s door.*

Exterior GRAYSON*'s room.*

GRAYSON *opens his door.*

GRAYSON: Oh hello. Sorry, are we making too much noise?

ANDERSON: No, it's all right, but I heard you were still up and I wondered if I could ask a favour of you. I wonder if I could borrow your typewriter.

GRAYSON: My typewriter?

ANDERSON: Yes.

GRAYSON: Well, I'm leaving in the morning.

ANDERSON: I'll let you have it back first thing. I'm leaving on the afternoon plane myself.

GRAYSON: Oh – all right then.

ANDERSON: That's most kind.

(During the above the voices from the room have been semi-audible. MCKENDRICK*'s voice, rather drunk, but articulate, is heard.)*

MCKENDRICK: (*His voice only, heard underneath the above dialogue*) Now, listen to me, I'm a professional philosopher. You'll do well to listen to what I have to say.

ANDERSON: That sounds as if you've got McKendrick in there.

GRAYSON: Oh – is he one of yours?

ANDERSON: I wouldn't put it like that.

GRAYSON: He's getting as tight as a tick.

ANDERSON: Yes.

GRAYSON: You couldn't collect him, could you? He's going to get clouted in a minute.

ANDERSON: Go ahead and clout him, if you like.

GRAYSON: It's not me. It's Broadbent and a couple of the lads. Your pal sort of latched on to us in the bar. He really ought to be getting home.

ANDERSON: I'll see what I can do.

(ANDERSON *follows* GRAYSON *into the room.*)

MCKENDRICK: How can you expect the kids to be little gentlemen when their heroes behave like yobs – answer me that – no – you haven't answered my question – if you've got yobs on the fields you're going to have yobs on the terraces.

(*Interior* GRAYSON*'s room.*

MCKENDRICK *is the only person standing up. He is holding court, with a bottle of whisky in one hand and his glass in the other. Around this small room are* BROADBENT, CRISP, CHAMBERLAIN, *and perhaps one or two members of the England squad. Signs of a bottle party.*)

GRAYSON: (*Closing his door*) I thought philosophers were quiet, studious sort of people.

ANDERSON: Well, some of us are.

MCKENDRICK: (*Shouts*) Anderson! You're the very man I want to see! We're having a philosophical discussion about the yob ethics of professional footballers –

BROADBENT: You want to watch it, mate.

MCKENDRICK: Roy here is sensitive because he gave away a penalty today, by a deliberate foul. To stop a certain goal he hacked a chap down. After all, a penalty might be saved and broken legs are quite rare –

(BROADBENT *stands up but* MCKENDRICK *pacifies him with a gesture.*)

it's perfectly all right – you were adopting the utilitarian values of the game, for the good of the team, for England! But I'm not talking about particular acts of expediency. No, I'm talking about the whole *ethos*.

ANDERSON: McKendrick, don't you think, it's about time we retired?

MCKENDRICK: (*Ignoring him*) Now, I've played soccer for years. Years and *years*. I played soccer from the age of *eight* until I was *thirteen*. At which point I went to a rugger school. Even so, Tommy here will tell you that I still consider myself something of a left winger. (*This is to* CRISP). Sorry about that business in the lift, by the way, Tommy. Well, one thing I remember clearly from my years and *years* of soccer is that if two players go for a ball which then goes into touch, there's never any doubt *among those players* which of them touched the ball last. I can't remember one occasion in all those years and *years* when the player who touched the ball last didn't realize it. So, what I want to know *is* – why is it that on Match of the Day, every time the bloody ball goes into touch, *both* players claim the throw-in for their own side? I merely ask for information. Is it because they are very, very stupid or is it because a dishonest advantage is as welcome as an honest one?

CHAMBERLAIN: Well, look, it's been a long evening, old chap –

ANDERSON: Tomorrow is another day, McKendrick.

MCKENDRICK: Tomorrow, in my experience, is usually the same day. Have a drink –

ANDERSON: No thank you.

MCKENDRICK: Here's a question for anthropologists. Name me a tribe which organizes itself into teams for sporting encounters and greets every score against their opponents with paroxysms of childish glee, whooping, dancing and embracing in an ecstasy of crowing self-congratulation in the very midst of their disconsolate fellows? – Who are these primitives who pile all their responses into the immediate sensation, unaware or uncaring of the long undulations of life's fortunes? Yes, you've got it! (*He chants the Match of the Day signature tune.*) It's the yob-of-the-month competition, entries on a postcard please. But the question is – is it because they're working class, or is it because financial greed has corrupted them? Or is it both?

ANDERSON: McKendrick, you are being offensive.

MCKENDRICK: Anderson is one of life's cricketers. Clap, clap. (*He claps in a well-bred sort of way and puts on a well-bred voice.*) Well played, sir. Bad luck, old chap. The comparison with cricket may suggest to you that yob ethics are working class.

(BROADBENT *comes up to* MCKENDRICK *and pushes him against the wall.* MCKENDRICK *is completely unconcerned, escapes and continues without pause.*)

But you would be quite wrong. Let me refer you to a typical rugby team of

Welsh miners. A score is acknowledged with pride but with restraint, the scorer himself composing his features into an expressionless mask lest he might be suspected of exulting in his opponents' misfortune – my God, it does the heart good, doesn't it? I conclude that yob ethics are caused by financial greed.

ANDERSON: Don't be such an ass.

(MCKENDRICK *takes this as an intellectual objection.*)

MCKENDRICK: You think it's the adulation, perhaps? (*To* CRISP.) Is it the adulation, Tommy, which has corrupted you?

CRISP: What's he flaming on about?

CHAMBERLAIN: Well I think it's time for my shut-eye.

CRISP: No, I want to know what he's saying about me. He's giving me the needle.

ANDERSON: (*To* MCKENDRICK) May I remind you that you profess to be something of a pragmatist yourself in matters of ethics –

MCKENDRICK: Ah yes – I see – you think that because I don't believe in reliable signposts on the yellow brick road to rainbowland, you think I'm a bit of a yob myself – the swift kick in the kneecap on the way up the academic ladder – the Roy Broadbent of Stoke – (*To* BROADBENT.) Stoke's my team, you know.

BROADBENT: Will you tell this stupid bugger his philosophy is getting up my nostrils.

GRAYSON: You're not making much sense, old boy.

MCKENDRICK: Ah! Grayson here has a fine logical mind. He has put his finger on the flaw in my argument, namely that the reason footballers are yobs may be nothing to do with being working class, or with financial greed, or with adulation, or even with being footballers. It may be simply that football attracts a certain kind of person, namely yobs –

(*This is as far as he gets when* BROADBENT *smashes him in the face.* MCKENDRICK *drops.*)

CRISP: Good on you, Roy.

(ANDERSON *goes to* MCKENDRICK *who is flat on the floor.*)

ANDERSON: McKendrick . . .

CHAMBERLAIN: Well, I'm going to bed.

(CHAMBERLAIN *goes through the connecting door into his own room and closes the door.*)

BROADBENT: He can't say that sort of thing and get away with it.

GRAYSON: Where's his room?

ANDERSON: On the third floor.

GRAYSON: Bloody hell.

CRISP: He's waking up.

BROADBENT: He's all right.

ANDERSON: Come on McKendrick.

(*They all lift* MCKENDRICK *to his feet.* MCKENDRICK *makes no protest. He's just about able to walk.*)

I'll take him down in the lift. (*He sees the typewriter in its case and says to* GRAYSON) I'll come back for the typewriter. (*He leads* MCKENDRICK *towards the door.*)

MCKENDRICK: (*Mutters*) All right. I went too far. Let's talk about something else.

(*But* MCKENDRICK *keeps walking or staggering.* ANDERSON *opens* GRAYSON*'s door.*)

BROADBENT: Here. That bloody Jirasek. Just like you said.

ANDERSON: Yes.

BROADBENT: They don't teach you nothing at that place then.

ANDERSON: No.

(ANDERSON *helps* MCKENDRICK *out and closes the door.*)

Conflict

1 The Birthday Party

Harold Pinter

Act Two

MCCANN *is sitting at the table tearing a sheet of newspaper into five equal strips. It is evening. After a few moments* STANLEY *enters from the left. He stops upon seeing* MCCANN, *and watches him. He then walks towards the kitchen, stops, and speaks.*

STANLEY: Evening.

MCCANN: Evening.

Chuckles are heard from outside the back door, which is open.

STANLEY: Very warm tonight. (*He turns towards the back door, and back.*) Someone out there?

MCCANN *tears another length of paper.* STANLEY *goes into the kitchen and pours a glass of water. He drinks it looking through the hatch. He puts the glass down, comes out of the kitchen and walks quickly towards the door, left.* MCCANN *rises and intercepts him.*

MCCANN: I don't think we've met.

STANLEY: No, we haven't.

MCCANN: My name's McCann.

STANLEY: Staying here long?

MCCANN: Not long. What's your name?

STANLEY: Webber.

MCCANN: I'm glad to meet you, sir. (*He offers his hand.* STANLEY *takes it, and* MCCANN *holds the grip.*) Many happy returns of the day. (STANLEY *withdraws his hand. They face each other.*) Were you going out?

STANLEY: Yes.

MCCANN: On your birthday?

STANLEY: Yes. Why not?

MCCANN: But they're holding a party here for you tonight.

STANLEY: Oh really? That's unfortunate.

MCCANN: Ah no. It's very nice.

Voices from outside the back door.

STANLEY: I'm sorry. I'm not in the mood for a party tonight.

MCCANN: Oh, is that so? I'm sorry.

STANLEY: Yes, I'm going out to celebrate quietly, on my own.

MCCANN: That's a shame.

They stand.

STANLEY: Well, if you'd move out of my way –

MCCANN: But everything's laid on. The guests are expected.

STANLEY: Guests? What guests?

MCCANN: Myself for one. I had the honour of an invitation.

MCCANN *begins to whistle 'The Mountains of Morne'.*

STANLEY (*moving away*). I wouldn't call it an honour, would you? It'll just be another booze-up.

STANLEY *joins* MCCANN *in whistling 'The Mountains of Morne'. During the next five lines the whistling is continuous, one whistling while the other speaks, and both whistling together.*

MCCANN: But it is an honour.

STANLEY: I'd say you were exaggerating.

MCCANN: Oh no, I'd say it was an honour.

STANLEY: I'd say that was plain stupid.

MCCANN: Oh no.

They stare at each other.

STANLEY: Who are the other guests?

MCCANN: A young lady.

STANLEY: Oh yes? And. . . .?

MCCANN: My friend.

STANLEY: Your friend?

2 A Visit from the Footbinder

Emily Prager

Wrinkled Linen

It was one of those days when they were fighting. After the news, they fought about where to eat dinner and he suggested the Russian Tea Room.

'I don't want to eat there,' she said, 'We have to get dressed up if we eat there and it's all the way uptown. Every time I go there I'm reminded of Christmas.'

'That's why I like it,' he said.

In the taxi going uptown, he noticed that she was wearing the pin he had given her for Christmas. She noticed that he had put on the birthday tie. This show of respect for each other's taste caused a momentary truce and they both leaned back against the leather Checker seats and decided to relax. They were friendly but silent until they reached the Port Authority Bus Terminal.

'God,' she said, rolling her eyeballs heavenward, 'I'm sorry, but I cannot believe how many homeless people are living on the streets of New York City. It's like Calcutta. Only in Calcutta it's families, in New York it's singles. Typical.'

'Yeah,' he said. 'There's a couple of old guys who live in front of the Greenwich Theatre. They hit me up for money every time I go by there.'

'And you always give it to them, don't you?' He nodded. 'I don't know why you're so big on giving derelicts money. What is it, luck? There but for the grace of God?'

'I'm a nice guy,' he said.

'You are a nice guy. No one's disputing that. I guess that makes me a lucky gal, doesn't it?'

'Yes,' he said, smiling, 'yes it does. You're a very lucky gal.'

'I used to have a girlfriend who always gave money to bums when she was between boyfriends and looking. She thought it would bring her luck in finding a fabulous guy.'

'Did it?' he asked.

'I don't know,' she replied. 'She's married a guy now but she isn't always happy.'

He said nothing. There was a silence as they both stared out the windows. She spoke first.

'What are you thinking?' she said.

'I'm thinking about dinner and what I'm going to eat. I'm hungry.'

She nodded wearily. 'Okay,' she sighed. 'Okay.'

'What?' he asked.

'Nothing, nothing. I just thought maybe you might be thinking about that last thing I said.'

'What?' he asked again.

'The thing about my friend who sometimes isn't happy and I thought you might be thinking, "Like us," because sometimes we fight.'

'No,' he said.

'No, what?' she asked.

'No, I wasn't thinking about that. I was thinking about dinner and what to order.'

'Great,' she said, sighing again. 'Great. Okay, so what are you having?'

'I don't know,' he said.

'Look,' she said, staring him in the eye, 'my parents didn't pay thousands of dollars for a fancy education for me to have conversations like this. I'm a verbal person. It said so on my kindergarten report. I must have discussions with others on topics of weight. How can I live with someone who never talks to me? It's like being in a Japanese hotbox in solitary confinement. I feel like my brain is starving to death for lack of human contact. The thing about Man is his power of speech. Do you understand wherefrom I'm coming, Mr No Mincing of Words?'

He looked petulant. 'We talk,' he said.

The cab pulled up in front of the Russian Tea Room and she got out, slamming the door behind her. She went through the revolving door and spoke to the maitre d'. When he came in, he joined her standing on the line.

'I just don't see what good it is having a successful boyfriend if he never talks to me,' she said.

'I can't just talk when you say talk. I'm spontaneous. And when you tell me to talk I clam up and it takes me some time to recover.'

'Can you talk now?' she asked.

'Not yet,' he answered and turned away.

'When? Soon?' she asked hopefully.

'Maybe,' he replied.

'Oh, look,' she exclaimed, quite excited, 'there's Sylvia Sidney!'

'Who?' he asked.

'Forget it,' she answered and kept silent until the maitre d' led them to the table.

He ordered the hot borscht and beef stroganoff. She ordered the chicken Kiev and the hot borscht. He would eat half of his piroshki. She would eat hers and the other half of his. He ordered a vodka gimlet and also ordered a bottle of wine for them to share.

'Now don't drink too much just because we're having a fight and you think you ought to drown your sorrows,' she said.

He gave her a sarcastic smile and took a big gulp of his drink.

'Okay, I get it, fuck you, Mom,' she said and didn't say another thing until the food came.

They were seated at one of the side tables for two, closed in on either side by other tables, excruciatingly close to their neighbours. The tablecloths were pink, as was the lighting, and Christmas balls and tinsel were in profusion even though it was summer. The décor had not changed in her entire life.

'You know,' she said, trying to start anew, 'I ate chicken Kiev here before I went to the first Beatles concert ever held in America, at Carnegie Hall in 1964. I had just finished eleventh grade.

'They were wearing sharkskin suits with velveteen lapels. Happy Rockefeller was in the first row and walked out in the middle, taking her kids with her. It was an event. To my knowledge there had never been a rock concert before. We screamed and got very excited. My friend DeeDee got us into the press conference after and we met them. Ringo said to me, "Don't we know you?" DeeDee had her picture taken with John. It was in the yearbook.'

'It must have been great,' he said.

'Yeah,' she said. 'The sixties. I adored the sixties. All my dreams came true in the sixties. I was blissfully happy. In the seventies, I had to recover from all that happiness. In the eighties, I'm finally a real person.'

He laughed. She continued.

'Something happened today that's made me understand the eighties: I was shopping and I came across these fabulous beige linen jodhpurs which I bought right away. I had vowed never to wear jodhpurs after seeing Elizabeth Taylor from behind in *Reflections in a Golden Eye*. But they look okay. They look good; I'm like a mini Ronald Reagan. Anyhow, linen is a classy material, really fine, and it was "in" when I was in high school too. We had linen dresses, and when you wore them, your whole life was about keeping them pressed and starched. Linen wrinkles like a motherfucker, but here's the thing, it was really low and slutty and ill-bred if you wore a linen dress with a wrinkle in it. I remember never sitting down, never raising my arms, and still always having wrinkles. So, today, I'm trying on these jodhpurs and I glance at the label and what do you think it says? "Guaranteed to Wrinkle." And I realized that's what the eighties is all about: off-colour coordinates. What do the eighties mean to you, Mr Snuggles?'

She smiled at him and went back to eating. He thought for a while and then said, 'The most freedom anyone's ever had while teetering on the edge of disaster.'

'On the edge of disaster? What do you mean by that?'

'Well, any minute the world could blow up,' he explained.

'Yeah? . . . Yeah?' She waited. 'Say more.'

He shrugged. 'No more. Want to see a movie after dinner?'

She seemed exasperated. 'I love the way you hasten from the cosmic to the particular. It keeps me on my toes. We could. We could see a movie, only . . .'

'Only what?'

'Only it's such an isolating experience seeing a movie.'

3 Twinkle, Twinkle, Little Spy

Len Deighton

Chapter Fifteen

Mann gave Mrs Bekuv no time to say goodbye to her husband: that was all part of his scheme. We sat in Mann's little office – originally intended for the duty nurse – and heard Andrei Bekuv walk down the corridor, calling his wife's name.

Mann sat hunched over a desk in the corner, watching the dark storm-clouds come racing in from the Atlantic. The rain beat upon the windows and the morning was so dark that Mann needed the desk light in order to read. He looked at me and winked as Andrei Bekuv came back.

'Here we go,' said Mann softly.

Andrei Bekuv was silhouetted against the brightness of the corridor lighting as he opened the door and looked in on us.

'Where is my wife, Major Mann? She wasn't at breakfast, and she's not swimming. Do you know where she has gone?'

'We've moved her to Baltimore,' said Mann without looking up from the papers he held under the desk light.

'When? When was this?' said Andrei Bekuv. He was jolted, and he scowled and looked at his watch. Bekuv was a creature of habit. Breakfast at seven, coffee at ten, a light lunch at one, dinner at seven thirty, in time for him to finish his meal and be in the armchair, with hi-fi tuned, ready for the evening concert. He insisted that the supply of vitamins in his medicine cabinet be replenished without his having to ask for them, and he liked decaffeinated coffee, served demi-tasse, in the evening, with fresh cream. And he liked to know where to find his wife.

'When?' repeated Bekuv.

'Oh, some time early this morning.' Mann turned the desk clock round to see it better. There was a barometer fitted into it and Mann tapped that. 'They should be there by now. Do you want to phone her?'

'Yes,' said Bekuv.

Mann picked up the phone and went through a pantomime of asking for a number in Baltimore. He thanked someone at the other end. And then hung up. 'Seems like we can't get through to Baltimore from here.'

'Why not?'

'I didn't think to ask. Do you want me to call the operator again?'

Bekuv came into the room and sat down. 'What game are you playing now, Major Mann?'

'I might ask you the same question, Professor Bekuv,' said Mann. From the clutter of papers and objects on the desk in front of him, Mann selected a large brown envelope. It contained something lumpy. He passed the envelope to Bekuv. 'Take a look at that, for example.'

Bekuv hesitated.

'Go ahead, take a look at it.'

Bekuv handled the envelope as if it might explode. I wondered afterwards if he guessed what was inside it. If he did, he was in no hurry to see it again. Finally, he ripped the edge of the envelope far enough to slide the contents out. There was a transparent plastic evidence bag with some typewritten labels attached to it. Inside the bag there was a flick-knife.

'The police sent that over here yesterday afternoon, Professor Bekuv. It was found near the steps of the church, during a search made during the early hours of Christmas morning. You remember Christmas morning?'

'It's the one used to wound my wife,' said Bekuv. He didn't open the bag. He dropped it back into the envelope as if it might have carried traces of some fatal contagion. He tried to pass the envelope back to Mann but the major would not accept it from him.

'That's right,' said Mann.

'What's it supposed to mean?' Bekuv demanded.

'Supposed to mean?' said Mann. 'I'm glad you said supposed to mean, because there's often a world of difference between what things mean, and what they are supposed to mean. For instance,' said Mann, 'that's the knife that caused your wife's wounds. Whether she was trying to knife you with it, or preventing you knifing her with it, or whether you were both trying to cut each other, or even turn it on yourselves, I wouldn't be too sure.'

'A man assaulted us,' said Bekuv.

'Yes, sure, that's the other theory isn't it? Didn't I mention that one? Forgive me.'

Bekuv looked at his watch. Whether he was thinking about his wife arriving in Baltimore, about his ten o'clock coffee or simply indulging in displacement activity that helped him gather his wits, there was no way of telling.

Mann picked up some papers from his desk, read for a moment or two and then said, 'Those gloves your wife was wearing . . . a shop in Fifth Avenue sells them for twenty-eight dollars a pair and advertises them as real kid, but in fact they make them from the skin of sheep. Now, that's the kind of dishonesty I hate. How about you, Professor?'

The professor did not commit himself: he grunted.

Mann said, 'Sheepskin. To make a pair of gloves like that the tanning process removes the epidermal layer . . .' Mann was reading from the paper '. . . to expose the corium minor or grain layer. It is the nature of this grain layer that enables a scientist to distinguish the age, sex and species of animal from which the skin originated.'

Professor Bekuv said, 'I'm not interested.'

'Hold on, Professor. I'm not through yet. It gets better. Did you know that the grain pattern from any piece of animal skin is as individual to that animal as a fingerprint is to one individual man?'

'What of it?'

'I'll tell you what of it,' said Mann. He put the papers back on his desk, turned to Bekuv and smiled. 'The police forensic lab took leather prints off that knife. They say it was wielded by your bride. They say her Fifth Avenue gloves left prints on that knife as clear and as evidential as if she'd used her bare hands.' Mann picked up another evidence bag that contained the gloves, and dropped it back on to the desk again. 'The police say your wife knifed herself, Professor. And they say they can prove it.'

Bekuv looked away.

'Anyway,' said Mann, breathing a sigh. 'The fact of the matter is that the investigation is closing as far as you are concerned. My people have lost interest in you – you've cost the American taxpayer too much money already. You'll be allowed to live wherever you like – within reason – but you'll have to find a place for yourself . . . the same goes for getting a job. No chair at N.Y.U. You will have to read the vacancies in the papers. For the time being the two of you are being kept separate but that's for your own protection. My people say that there will be more chance of your K.G.B. squads killing you if you are together. Next year, of course, the danger will have subsided a little. By then there will probably be no objection to your living under the same roof again.'

'Now wait a minute . . .' said Bekuv.

'Sorry it had to go this way, Professor. As your wife understood so well, this could have been a big one for us.' He smiled to show that he held no ill feelings. 'You'll be able to keep the hi-fi and the recordings and stuff of course.' He picked up papers from his desk and tapped them edge-down on the desk to tidy them.

It was only then that Bekuv seemed to become aware of my presence in the dark corner of the office. He turned to me. 'Is Miss Bancroft with my wife?' he asked.

'That's right,' I said. 'She'll be with her for a little while.'

'How long,' he said. 'I don't want my wife to be with Miss Bancroft.'

'No one tells me anything, Professor,' I said.

Mann said, 'Your wife wanted Miss Bancroft along for company.' Bekuv nodded. Mann had been making a great play of rummaging round his desk and, as Bekuv turned to leave, he suddenly produced a flimsy sheet of paper, waved it and said, 'Oh, this is something for you, Professor. It's a copy of a letter to your wife.'

He passed it to him. It was a carbon copy of a letter. There were a couple of official rubber stamps on it and a paper-clip. Bekuv took it without a word, and moved over to the window to read it by the grey morning light. He read it aloud in his careful English . . .

4 One Flew Over the Cuckoo's Nest

Ken Kesey

'Another thing: I'm in this place because that's the way I planned it, pure and simple, because it's a better place than a work farm. As near as I can tell I'm no looney, or never knew it if I was. Your nurse don't know this; she's not going to be looking out for somebody coming at her with a trigger-quick mind like I obviously got. These things give me an edge I like. So I'm saying five bucks to each of you that wants it if I can't put a betsy bug up that nurse's butt within a week.'

'I'm still not sure I –'

'Just that. A bee in her butt, a burr in her bloomers. Get her goat. Bug her till she comes apart at those neat little seams, and shows, just one time, she ain't so unbeatable as you think. One week. I'll let you be the judge whether I win or not.'

Harding takes out a pencil and writes something on the pinochle pad. 'Here. A lien on ten dollars of that money they've got drawing dust under my name over in Funds. It's worth twice that to me, my friend, to see this unlikely miracle brought off.'

McMurphy looks at the paper and folds it. 'Worth it to any of the rest of you birds?' Other Acutes line up now, taking turns at the pad. He takes the pieces of paper when they're finished, stacking them on his palm, pinned under a big stiff thumb. I see the pieces of paper crowd up in his hand. He looks them over.

'You trust me to hold the bets, buddies?'

'I believe we can be safe in doing that,' Harding says. 'You won't be going any place for a while.'

One Christmas at midnight on the button, at the old place, the ward door blows open with a crash, in comes a fat man with a beard, eyes ringed red by the cold and his nose just the colour of a cherry. The black boys get him cornered in the hall with flashlights. I see he's all tangled in the tinsel Public Relation has been stringing all over the place, and he's stumbling around in it in the dark. He's shading his red eyes from the flashlights and sucking on his mustache.

'Ho ho ho,' he says. 'I'd like to stay but I must be hurrying along. Very tight schedule, ya know. Ho ho. Must be going . . .'

The black boys move in with the flashlights. They kept him with us six years before they discharged him, clean-shaven and skinny as a pole.

The Big Nurse is able to set the wall clock at whatever speed she wants by just turning one of those dials in the steel door; she takes a notion to hurry things up, she turns the speed up, and those hands whip around that disc like spokes in a wheel. The scene in the picture-screen windows goes through rapid changes of light to show morning, noon, and night – throb off and on furiously with day and dark, and everybody is driven like mad to keep up with that passing of fake time; awful scramble of shaves and breakfasts and appointments and lunches and medications and ten minutes of night so you barely get your eyes closed before the dorm light's screaming at you to get up and start the scramble again, go like a sonofabitch this way, going through the full schedule of a day maybe twenty times an hour, till the Big Nurse sees everybody is right up to the breaking point, and she slacks off on the throttle, eases off the pace on that clock-dial, like some kid been fooling with the moving-picture projection machine and finally got tired watching the film run at ten times its natural speed, got bored with all that silly scampering and insect squeak of talk and turned it back to normal.

She's given to turning up the speed this way on days like, say, when you got somebody to visit you or when the VFW brings down a smoker show from Portland – times like that, times you'd like to hold and have stretch out. That's when she speeds things up.

But generally it's the other way, the slow way. She'll turn that dial to a dead stop and freeze the sun there on the screen so it don't move a scant hair for weeks, so not a leaf on a tree or a blade of grass in the pasture shimmers. The clock hands hang at two minutes to three and she's liable to let them hang there till we rust. You sit solid and you can't budge, you can't walk or move to relieve the strain of sitting, you can't swallow and you can't breathe. The only thing you can move is your eyes and there's nothing to see but petrified Acutes across the room waiting on one another to decide whose play it is. The old Chronic next to me has been dead six days, and he's rotting to the chair. And instead of fog sometimes she'll let a clear chemical gas in through the vents, and the whole ward is set solid when the gas changes into plastic.

Lord knows how long we hang this way.

Then, gradually, she'll ease the dial up a degree, and that's worse yet. I can take hanging dead still better'n I can take that sirup-slow hand of Scanlon across the room, taking three days to lay down a card. My lungs pull for the thick plastic air like getting in through a pinhole. I try to go to the latrine and I feel buried under a ton of sand, squeezing my bladder till green sparks flash and buzz across my forehead.

I strain with every muscle and bone to get out of that chair and go to the latrine, work to get up till my arms and legs are all ashake and my teeth hurt. I pull and pull and all I gain is maybe a quarter-inch off the leather seat. So I fall back and give up and let the pee pour out, activating a hot salt wire down my left leg that sets off humiliating alarms, sirens, spotlights, everybody up yelling and running around and the big black boys knocking the crowd aside right and left as the both of them rush headlong at me, waving awful mops of wet copper wires cracking and spitting as they short with the water.

About the only time we get any let-up from this time control is in the fog; then time doesn't mean anything. It's lost in the fog, like everything else. (They haven't really fogged the place full force all day today, not since McMurphy came in. I bet he'd yell like a bull if they fogged it.)

When nothing else is going on, you usually got the fog or the time control to contend with, but today something's happened: there hasn't been any of these things worked on us all day, not since shaving. This afternoon everything is matching up. When the swing shift comes on duty the clock says four-thirty, just like it should. The Big Nurse dismisses the black boys and takes a last look around the ward. She slides a long silver hatpin out of the iron-blue knot of hair back of her head, takes off her white cap and sets it careful in a cardboard box (there's mothballs in that box), and drives the hatpin back in the hair with a stab of her hand.

Behind the glass I see her tell everyone good evening. She hands the little birthmarked swing-shift nurse a note; then her hand reaches out to the control panel in the steel door, clacks on the speaker in the day room: 'Good evening, boys. Behave yourselves.' And turns the music up louder than ever. She rubs the inside of her wrist across her window; a disgusted look shows the fat black boy who just reported on duty that he better get to cleaning it, and he's at the glass with a paper towel before she's so much as locked the ward door behind her.

The machinery in the walls whistles, sighs, drops into a lower gear.

Then, till night, we eat and shower and go back to sit in the day room. Old Blastic, the oldest Vegetable, is holding his stomach and moaning. George (the black boys call him Rub-a-dub) is washing his hands in the drinking fountain. The Acutes sit and play cards and work at getting a picture on our TV set by carrying the set every place the cord will reach, in search of a good beam.

5 On the Yankee Station

William Boyd

Lydecker had expected the insults, the dirty jobs and the regular appearance on charge sheets to die down after Pfitz had flown a few more missions, but if anything they intensified. Soon Lydecker came to see that the old Crusader was acting as a catalyst, a regular reminder of Pfitz's shame. Every time the Crusader was towed out amongst the Phantoms and the Skyhawks Pfitz remembered all the details of that day: watching his new plane scythe cleanly into the waves, the hours of subjective time as he gently floated down into the sea, the rows of incredulous grinning faces as the rescue helicopter deposited him back on board, the sly jibes and quips of his fellow officers in the mess-rooms. And each time he climbed into the cockpit, saw the unfamiliar instrument layout and the dated mechanisms, the shame returned. And as he pulled away from the ship on a mission he imagined it brazenly echoing to the crews' gleeful laughter. And every time he took the Crusader up and landed Lydecker was there, the man who'd caused the foul-up, weasely shit-face Lydecker, draining the fuel tanks or fitting the chocks to the wheels. And then Pfitz would claim his cannon misfired or the fuel-flow was imbalanced and he'd put him on a charge for slipshod work, or kick his narrow butt the length of the repair bay, or assign him to descale the afterburner all night.

For Lydecker the one benefit of the whole thing was the Crusader. His first posting had been to a 6th fleet carrier in the Mediterranean that still had a squadron of Crusaders in operation. He had grown familiar with the planes and had an affection for them that he did not bestow on the lean Phantoms or the dainty Skyhawks. The Crusader was a hefty rectangular machine, large for a single seater, with the crude geometry of a bus. Its single intake was set in the nose, like a gaping mouth beneath the matt black cone that housed the radar. It was like greeting an old friend when Pfitz's was wheeled out from storage and hoisted up to the deck. Its strong unambiguous profile seemed to render the other planes less significant and somehow pretentious. Pfitz was loudly derogatory, complaining that she was a pig to fly and sluggish to manoeuvre. But then he soon discovered in it other qualities which he employed in wreaking his revenge on the population of Vietnam.

The payload of the Crusader was prodigious; its sturdy frame could carry an anthology of destructive weaponry beneath its wings. Pfitz was highly satisfied with this aspect, soon indifferent to the absence of computer technology that precluded him from carrying laser or guided bombs like the Phantoms. And he was never happier than when he supervised his crew as they bolted the finless cigar-shaped canisters of napalm to the underwing pylons. Pasquale overheard him talking about a request he'd made to be excused the carrying of all other bomb loads and how he'd voluntarily restricted himself to napalm. He started to refer to his aircraft as the 'Rose Train' and had Huq, who was something of an artist, paint this below his cockpit.

'It's like roses in the jungle, man,' he would crow on returning from a mission. 'You see them cans tumblin' and whoomph, it's like a fuckin great flower bloomin in the trees – wham, pink an' orange roses. Beautiful man, just beautiful.' He made Huq keep a tally of missions by painting a red rose beneath the cockpit sill.

Lydecker thought he had gone mad, and so did many of the other pilots. Napalm had to be delivered from low level making the plane vulnerable to ground fire. With half a dozen canisters wobbling like overripe fruit beneath your wings you could be transformed into a comet of blazing petroleum jelly with one lucky shot. Lydecker sometimes thought about this as he patched bullet holes in the wings and tail.

Often at night Lydecker would leave the brightly lit crew quarters, where the air was thick with smoke, and bored sailors played cards or told obscene stories, and wander up to the dark cavern of the main hangar below the deck where the atmosphere had a tranquil metallic chill and the smell of oil and engine coolant clung to the air. He would go over to the Crusader, ponderously low slung on its curious trolley undercarriage that jutted like spavined legs from the fuselage belly, and run his hands over the scarred and chipped aluminium, his fingers tracing and caressing the lines of rivet heads. Like the hated bullied schoolchild who tinkers with his bike all day Lydecker enjoyed the mute presence of his plane. It was like some gigantic familiar toy, stored in a cupboard with its wings folded and canopy up. He knew every square centimetre of the plane, from its gaping intake to the scorched jet at the rear. He had clambered all over its body, fuelling and rearming it, riveting patches of aluminium alloy over the puckered ulcers caused by random bullets. He had climbed into the dark ventral recesses of the undercarriage bay checking the hydraulic system, and had inched along its ribbed length replacing frayed control wires and realigning the armour plate. And he found himself, like an anxious mother, fretting for its return after long missions to Laos or Haiphong.

The war was a distant affair to the men on the 'Yankee Station' in the South China Sea. Just a green haze on the horizon sometimes. Even for the pilots who flew above it, dumping tons of high explosive on the jungle, the war and the enemy remained abstract and remote. To them it was a dangerous demanding job and only Pfitz openly expressed the requisite warlike antagonism; only he seemed to be exulted by the regular missions and the crop of red roses that grew on the side of the plane.

Then one late afternoon a seabird was sucked into the intake as the Crusader came in to land.

Dilemmas

1 A Dream of Africa
Camara Laye

A sleepless night

I still had not reached my twentieth birthday when I left my native land for the first time.

One leaden evening, when the sun's rays were only just managing to pierce a thick mist, the 'plane on the regular Air France flight was circling very low over the Paris suburbs, preparing to land. Sunk in their seats, safety-belts fastened, the passengers, with bated breath, were awaiting the end of their long journey from Africa.

Finally, the great metal bird had touched down; then it had trundled rather rapidly towards a horizon barred by tall houses. Afterwards, losing speed, it had turned, had followed a flare-path that took a turn to the right, another to the left, and had come to a halt in front of the immense buildings of Orly Airport. The passengers, conducted by hostesses, had almost immediately taken seats in a bus going to the Invalides.

That was the evening on which I experienced the cold for the first time, that horrible cold which until then I had known only through books, a purely theoretical knowledge therefore; but now, this was the real thing stinging my eyes and freezing my ears . . .

'Don't curl up! Keep moving!' had been the advice given me by a young man seated next to me who seemed alarmed when he saw me with my shoulders up to my ears under the cruel cold.

'Well, it's far from warm in here!' I had replied briefly. He did not give me any further advice.

The young man, probably a Parisian, seemed to be familiar with the region; with his face glued to the window throughout the trip, he kept murmuring the names of villages on the outskirts of Paris, names which the spasmodic roaring of the engine prevented me from hearing distinctly.

The Invalides at last! . . . Everyone started bustling around, and I got pushed about; everyone had to carry his own luggage to the waiting taxis.

It was strange, because that evening no one had come to meet me. Perhaps the cable despatched from Africa had been delayed. But by a fortunate coincidence I had met a young African, who, I had been told at home, was studying law at Grenoble. He was called Diabaté. His nonchalant manner revealed that he was perfectly accustomed to Parisian life, to this hubbub, to these milling crowds, and above all to the cold. I had given him my name: Fatoman.

'Where are you going, Fatoman?' he asked. 'Are they expecting you in the provinces?'

'Yes, Argenteuil.'

'Argenteuil,' he declared, 'is not the provinces, but a suburb close, very close, to where we are now. You'll have no difficulty getting there. Just take the metro there, over the road.'

But he had guessed that I was having trouble following his explanations. It could be seen on my face. So he had gone on:

'Look! Go down that hole there, just over there, and follow the crowd . . . Then, at the Gare Saint-Lazare, you can catch your train for Argenteuil.'

He shook my hand, then vanished in the throng, for he told me he was in a hurry to catch the first available train to Grenoble.

After Diabaté had taken leave of me thus, I was left alone, depairingly alone, my bags and possessions scattered at random round my feet. And suddenly my thoughts had returned to the scene my mother had made the evening before, arguing with me and with my father to prevent my departure:

'Will I never have any peace of mind? . . . Yesterday it was a school in Conakry; today, it's a school in France. Tomorrow . . . who knows what it'll be tomorrow? Every day another new caper to take my son away from me! . . . Have you already forgotten how ill he was at Conakry, poor little thing?' she had added, turning on my father. 'But no, you're never content! It's sending him to France you're after now. Are you mad? Or do you want to drive *me* mad? And as for you,' she cried, wheeling upon me, 'you're nothing but a thankless child. Any excuse is good enough for you to run away from your mother. Only this time, it's not going to be as you imagine it's going to be, not by a long chalk!' And raising her eyes she had addressed the heavens: 'So many years already I've been parted from my boy!'

My thoughts continued to roam: I remembered my uncles, who had treated me in such a friendly, affectionate way; my imagination embraced the years to come, my future passions. And suddenly I felt happy, despite my loneliness . . .

2 The British Museum is Falling Down

David Lodge

There was one feature of his diurnal pilgrimage to the British Museum that afforded Adam a modest but constant gratification, and that was the fact that, as a familiar figure, he was not asked to show his card on entering the Reading Room. When he passed the doorkeeper with just a nod of greeting he assumed, he hoped, an air of importance for the group of casual visitors who invariably hung about outside the door, trying to peer into the Reading Room.

'Could I see your card, sir?'

Adam, his hand already on the swing door, halted and looked with astonishment and hurt pride at the doorkeeper, who grinned and pointed to a notice requesting all readers to show their cards that day.

'The annual check, sir,' he said, taking Adam's card from his hand. 'Ah, two months out of date. I'm afraid you'll have to go and renew it.'

'Oh look, I'm late as it is this morning. Can't I do it after I've ordered my books?'

'Sorry, sir.'

Adam dropped his bags with an angry thud at the feet of an Easter Island god, and stumped off to renew the ticket. Near the Elgin Marbles was a heavy door, guarded by a stern-looking porter with a huge key. When notified of Adam's errand, this official grudgingly unlocked the door, and ushered him into a long corridor. He then rang a little bell, and went out again, *locking the door behind him.*

Adam, or A as he would now more vaguely have identified himself, had been all through this before, but could not be sure whether he had dreamed it or actually experienced it. He was trapped. Behind him was a locked, guarded door; in front of him a long corridor terminating in a room. He could not go back. He could not stay where he was – the men in the room at the end of the corridor, warned by the bell, were expecting him. He went reluctantly forward, down the long corridor, between the smooth polished wooden cabinets, locked and inscrutable, which formed the walls, stretching high out of reach. Craning his neck to see if they reached the high ceiling, A felt suddenly dizzy, and leaned against the wall for support.

The room at the end of the corridor was an office, with a long, curving counter behind which sat two men, neat, self-possessed, expectant. A approached the nearer man, who immediately began writing on a piece of paper.

'Yes?' he said, after a few minutes had passed, and without looking up.

A, his mouth unaccountably dry, enunciated with difficulty the words, 'Reading Room Ticket.'

'Over there.'

A sidled along the counter to the second man, who immediately began writing in a ledger. A waited patiently.

'Yes?' said the second man, closing his ledger with a snap that made A jump.

'IwanttorenewmyReadingRoomTicket,' gabbled A.

'Over there.'

'But I've just been over there. He sent me to you.' Out of the corner of his eye, A saw the first man watching them intently.

The second man scrutinized him for what seemed a very long time, then spoke. 'One moment.' He went over to the first man, and they held a whispered conference, at the conclusion of which the first man came over to A and sat down in the second man's seat.

'What is it you want, exactly?' he asked.

'I want to renew my Reading Room Ticket,' said A patiently.

'You want to *renew* it? You mean you have a ticket already?'

'Yes.'

'May I see it?'

A presented his ticket.

'It's out of date,' observed the man.

'That's why I want to renew it!' A exclaimed.

'When did you last use the Reading Room?'

'Two months ago,' lied A, cunningly.

'You haven't used it since your ticket expired?'

'No.'

'It wouldn't matter if you had,' said the man. 'As long as you're not lying.' He tore A's ticket neatly into four sections, and deposited them in a waste-paper basket. It distressed A to see his ticket torn up. He experienced a queasy, empty feeling in his stomach.

'So now you want to renew your annual ticket?'

'Please.'

'You see, you didn't make that clear to me just now.'

'I'm sorry.'

'I assumed you were a casual reader wanting a short-term ticket. That's why I sent you to my colleague.' He nodded in the direction of the second man. 'But when he realized you wanted an annual ticket, he directed you back to me. That is the reason for our apparently contradictory behaviour.'

He flashed a sudden smile, displaying a row of gold-filled teeth.

'I see. I'm afraid it was my fault,' A apologized.

'Don't mention it,' said the first man, opening the ledger and beginning to write.

'Could I have my new ticket now?' said A, after some minutes had passed.

'Over there.'

'But you just said you were responsible for renewing annual tickets!' protested A.

'Ah, but that was when I was sitting over there,' said the first man. 'We've changed places now. We do that from time to time. So that if one of us should fall ill,' he continued, 'the other can cover his work.'

A made his way wearily to the second man.

'Good morning. Can I help you?' said the second man, as if greeting him for the first time.

'I want to renew my annual Reading Room ticket,' said A.

'Certainly. May I see your old ticket?'

'No, the other man – gentleman – has just torn it up.'

'It *was* an annual ticket you had?'

'Yes. He just tore it up. Didn't you see him?'

The second man shook his head gravely. 'This is very irregular. You shouldn't have given him the ticket. He's on short-term tickets now.'

'Look, all I want is to have my ticket renewed. What does it matter which of you does it?'

'I'm afraid I can't renew a ticket which, as far as I'm concerned, doesn't exist.'

A gripped the counter tightly and closed his eyes. 'What do you suggest I do then?' he whispered hoarsely.

'I could give you a short-term ticket . . .'

'No that won't do. I'm working here every day. My livelihood depends upon my being here every day.'

'Then I can only suggest that you come back when my colleague and I have changed places again,' said the second man.

'When will that be?'

'Oh there's no telling. You can wait if you like . . . in that room over there . . . you'll find plenty of people to chat to while you're waiting . . . your name will be called . . .'

3 A Man For All Seasons

Robert Bolt

MARGARET: I've not yet told you what the house is like, without you.

MORE: Don't, Meg.

MARGARET: What we do in the evenings, now that you're not there.

MORE: Meg, have done!

MARGARET: We sit in the dark because we've no candles. And we've no talk because we're wondering what they're doing to you here.

3 Unreliable Memoirs

Clive James

Toys were scarce. A few crude lead soldiers were still produced so that children could go on poisoning themselves but otherwise there was almost nothing. It was a big event when my mother bought me a little painted red cow. Presumably it was English. I took it to school and lost it. Next day she came with me to school, wanting to find out what had happened to it. My carelessness with everything she bought me went on hurting her for years. She construed it, accurately, as ingratitude. From the sensitivity angle I was about as obtuse as a child can be. I was sensitive enough about myself, but that's a different thing.

School, passable for the first year, became unbearable in the second, when the kind Miss Dear was supplanted by a hard case called Miss Turnbull. Dark, cold and impatient, Miss Turnbull might have been the firm hand I needed, but already I was unable to cope with authority. I still can't today, tending to oscillate between nervous flippancy and overly solicitous respect. In those days, when I was about a third of my present height and a quarter of the weight, there was nothing to do except duck. I did everything to get out of facing up to Miss Turnbull. I had Mondayitis every day of the week. As my mother dragged me down the front path, I would clutch my stomach, cross my eyes, stick out my tongue, cough, choke, scream and vomit simultaneously.

But there were some occasions when I ended up at school no matter what I did. It was then revealed that I had Dropped Behind the Class. Words I could not recognize would come up on the spelling wheel. The spelling wheel was a thick card with a window in it and a cardboard disc behind. As you turned the disc, words appeared one at a time in the window. I remember not being able to pronounce the word 'the'. I pronounced it 'ter-*her*'. The class had collective hysterics. They were rolling around on the floor with their knees up. I suppose one of the reasons why I grew up feeling the need to cause laughter was perpetual fear of being its unwitting object.

From the start of Miss Turnbull's reign until the day we left Jannali, every morning I would shout the house down. For my mother, the path leading from the front porch to the front gate became a Via Dolorosa. My act reached ever new heights of extravagance. Either it worked or it didn't. If it didn't I would sit in school praying for the bushfires to come early and incinerate the place. If it did I would either hang around the house or go and play with Ron, a truant of my own age who lived next to Hally the butcher down near the station. Ron was a grub. I was always being warned off him because he was so filthy. He and I used to squat under his house tweaking each other's ding, watching each other pee, and so on. I can't remember it all now. I suppose I have repressed it. If there was any sexual excitement, it took the form of intense curiosity, just as I was curious about my mother when we were in the bath together. I remembered the shock of seeing Ray undressed. He looked as if he had a squirrel hanging there. I had an acorn.

MORE: The King's more merciful than you. He doesn't use the rack.

[*Enter* JAILER.]

JAILER: Two minutes to go, sir. I thought you'd like to know.

MORE: Two minutes!

JAILER: Till seven o'clock, sir. Sorry. Two minutes.

[*Exit* JAILER.]

MORE; Jailer – ! [*Seizes Roper by the arm.*] Will – go to him, talk to him, keep him occupied – [*Propelling him after Jailer.*]

ROPER: How, sir?

MORE: Anyhow! – Have you got any money?

ROPER [*eager*]: Yes!

MORE: No, don't try and bribe him! Let him play for it; he's got a pair of dice. And talk to him, you understand! And take this [*the wine*] – and mind you share it – do it properly, Will!

[ROPER *nods vigorously and exits.*]

Now listen, you must leave the country. All of you must leave the country.

MARGARET: And leave you here?

MORE: It makes no difference, Meg; they won't let you see me again. [*Breathlessly, a prepared speech under pressure*] You must all go on the same day, but not on the same boat; different boats from different ports –

MARGARET: After the trial, then.

MORE: There'll be no trial, they have no case. Do this for me I beseech you?

MARGARET: Yes.

MORE: Alice? [*She turns her back.*] Alice, I command it!

ALICE [*harshly*]: Right!

MORE [*looks into basket*]: Oh, this is splendid; I know who packed this.

ALICE [*harshly*]: I packed it.

MORE: Yes. [*Eats a morsel.*] You still make superlative custard, Alice.

ALICE: Do I?

MORE: That's a nice dress you have on.

ALICE: It's my cooking dress.

MORE: It's very nice anyway. Nice colour.

ALICE [*turns; quietly*]: By God, you think very little of me. [*with mounting bitterness*] I know I'm a fool. But I'm no such fool as at this time to be lamenting for my dresses! Or to relish complimenting on my custard!

[MORE *regards her with frozen attention. He nods once or twice.*]

MORE: I am well rebuked. [*Holds out his hands.*] Al –!

ALICE: No! [*She remains where she is, glaring at him.*]

MORE [*he is in great fear of her*]: I am faint when I think of the worst that they may do to me. But worse than that would be to go, with you not understanding why I go.

ALICE: I don't!

MORE [*just hanging on to his self-possession*]: Alice, if you can tell me that you understand, I think I can make a good death, if I have to.

ALICE: Your death's no 'good' to me!

MORE: Alice, you must tell me that you understand!

ALICE: I don't! [*She throws it straight at his head.*] I don't believe this had to happen.

MORE [*his face is drawn*]: If you say that, Alice, I don't see how I'm to face it.

ALICE: It's the truth!

MORE [*gasping*]: You're an honest woman.

ALICE: Much good may it do me! I'll tell you what I'm afraid of; that when you've gone, I shall hate you for it.

[MORE *turns from her: his face working.*]

MORE: Well, you mustn't, Alice, that's all.

[*Swiftly she crosses the stage to him; he turns and they clasp each other fiercely.*]

You mustn't, you –

ALICE [*covers his mouth with her hand*]: S-s-sh . . . As for understanding, I understand you're the best man that I ever met or am likely to; and if you go – well God knows why I suppose – though as God's my witness God's kept deadly quiet about it! And if anyone wants my opinion of the King and his Council they've only to ask for it!

MORE: Why, it's a lion I married! A lion! A lion! [*He breaks away from her, his face shining.*] Get them to take half this to Bishop Fisher – they've got him in the upper gallery –

ALICE: It's for you, not Bishop Fisher!

MORE: Now do as I ask – [*Breaks off a piece of the custard and eats it.*]

Oh, it's good, it's very, very good.

[*He puts his face in his hands;* ALICE *and* MARGARET *comfort him;* ROPER *and* JAILER *erupt on to the stage above, wrangling fiercely.*]

JAILER: It's no good, sir! I know what you're up to! And it can't be done!

ROPER: Another minute, man!

JAILER [*to* MORE *descending*]: Sorry, sir, time's up!

ROPER [*gripping his shoulder from behind*]: For pity's sake –!

JAILER [*shaking him off*]: Now don't do that, sir! Sir Thomas, the ladies will have to go now!

MORE: You said seven o'clock!

JAILER: It's seven now. You must understand my position, sir.

MORE: But one more minute!

MARGARET: Only a little while – give us a little while!

JAILER [*reproving*]: Now, Miss, you don't want to get me into trouble.

ALICE: Do as you're told. Be off at once!

[*The first stroke of seven is heard on a heavy, deliberate bell, which continues, reducing what follows to a babble.*]

JAILER [*taking* MARGARET *firmly by the upper arm*]: Now come along, Miss; you'll get your father into trouble as well as me.

[ROPER *descends and grabs him.*]

Are you obstructing me, sir?

[MARGARET *embraces* MORE, *and dashes up the stairs and exits, followed by* ROPER. JAILER *takes Alice gingerly by the arm.*]

Now, my lady, no trouble!

ALICE [*throwing him off as she rises*]: *Don't* put your muddy hand on me!

JAILER: Am I to call the guard then? Then come on!

[ALICE, *facing him, puts foot on bottom stair and so retreats before him, backwards.*]

MORE: For God's sake, man, we're saying good-bye!

JAILER: You don't know what you're asking, sir. You don't know how you're watched.

ALICE: Filthy, stinking, gutter-bred turnkey!

JAILER: Call me what you like, ma'am; you've got to go.

ALICE: I'll see you suffer for this!

JAILER: You're doing your husband no good!

MORE: Alice, good-bye, my love!

[*On this, the last stroke of the seven sounds.* ALICE *raises her hand, turns, and, with considerable dignity, exits.* JAILER *stops at head of stairs and addresses* MORE, *who, still crouching, turns from him, facing audience.*]

JAILER [*reasonably*]: You understand my position, sir, there's nothing I can do; I'm a plain simple man and just want to keep out of trouble.

MORE [*cries out passionately*]: Oh, Sweet Jesus! These plain, simple, men!

4 Forty Years On

Alan Bennett

Extract A

COUNSEL: Mr Chamberlain. You are charged that on the night of September 30th, 1938, you did indecently expose yourself at the windows of your home, No. 10 Downing Street, clad only in a scrap of paper and shouting 'Peace With Honour', 'Peace with Honour'. How say you, guilty or not guilty?

CHAMBERLAIN: I'm not sure.

JUDGE: Mr Chamberlain. You are either guilty or not guilty. That is something you must decide for yourself. The Court cannot decide it for you.

CHAMBERLAIN: I thought that was what courts were for.

JUDGE: Don't be impertinent or I shall have you smacked on the back of your legs. I shall now proceed to the sentence. [*Drum roll.*]

COUNSEL: But the evidence, m'lud.

JUDGE: The prisoner has come here for sentence. Let us get that out of the way before we hear the evidence. First things first.

COUNSEL: It's usual to have the evidence first, m'lud.

JUDGE: Don't try to tie me up in legal mumbo jumbo. I know the trial procedure backwards.

COUNSEL: On a point of law, m'lud, the defendant has his umbrella in the dock.

JUDGE: So he does. Are you expecting rain, Mr Chamberlain?

CHAMBERLAIN: No, m'lud.

JUDGE: Because I must warn you that in this court rain does not fall on the just and on the unjust but solely and indeed heavily upon the latter. Proceed.

COUNSEL: The charge arises out of a visit made by the accused to Munich to see Herr Hitler in the autumn of 1938.

CHAMBERLAIN: By aeroplane.

COUNSEL: What has that got to do with it?

CHAMBERLAIN: I went by aeroplane. I was sixty-nine. I had never flown in my life before. I was the first Prime Minister ever to fly.

COUNSEL: That may be the substance of a small footnote in the history of aeronautics but it is of no relevance to the court of history. What was your occupation at the time the offence was committed?

CHAMBERLAIN: Prime Minister and Leader of the Conservative Party.

COUNSEL: Prime Minister *and* Leader of the Conservative Party. You were doing two jobs?

CHAMBERLAIN: There was very little distinction between them.

COUNSEL: There was very little distinction between them. That was partly the trouble, wasn't it?

JUDGE: Oh, you're excelling yourself, Mr Witty. You'll have to do better than this, Mr Chamberlain.

COUNSEL: Let us look at Herr Hitler. You are not blind, your eyesight is not defective . . . it must have been perfectly obvious Herr Hitler wore a moustache.

CHAMBERLAIN: Yes, I did notice that.

COUNSEL: You did notice it, I see. You did not, I take it, recall that Kaiser Wilhelm, one of the prime causes of the First War, also had a moustache?

CHAMBERLAIN: Yes.

COUNSEL: Mr Chamberlain, do you learn nothing from history?

JUDGE: You're getting into your stride, Mr Witty. You're going to have to pull something out of the bag very soon, Mr Chamberlain.

COUNSEL: Getting back to Herr Hitler. It must have been obvious to anyone that he was a patent scallywag.

CHAMBERLAIN: He was not a gentleman certainly, but he was very fond of dogs.

COUNSEL: For sovereign states to conclude agreements on the basis of a mutual fondness for dogs seems to me to be barking up the wrong tree.

CHAMBERLAIN: But it was what the people wanted.

COUNSEL: The law of history is not a law of supply and demand, Mr Chamberlain.

CHAMBERLAIN: They were dancing in the streets.

COUNSEL: Dancing in the streets, what has that got to do with it. The purpose of international relations is not simply to enable the idle populace to take to the streets and do the fox-trot.

JUDGE: What is the fox-trot?

[COUNSEL *seizes* MISS NISBITT, *and they dance as the boys sing a snatch of 'Boom, why did my heart go boom?'*]

Extract B

JUDGE: Thank you, Mr Chamberlain. You seem to me if I may say so . . . and since I am the Judge I may say so . . . a man of the most frivolous mind.

CHAMBERLAIN: Beg pardon.

JUDGE: You forget, this is a court of history and we do not repeat ourselves.

COUNSEL: What consequences had this crime? Did it not lead to the rape of Czechoslovakia?

JUDGE: Oh, goody! A witness! Is Czechoslovakia in the court?

[MISS NISBITT *enters, draped in a sash, representing* CZECHOSLOVAKIA.]

Ah, charming, charming. You say you were raped, my dear?

CZECHOSLOVAKIA: Yes, m'lud.

JUDGE: You suprise me. Proceed.

COUNSEL: I'm going to ask you for evidence of identification. Can you see the guilty party in the court?

CZECHOSLOVAKIA: Yes. [*She points at the* AUDIENCE.]

JUDGE: No, my dear. That is the jury. And it is one of the most cherished maxims of English law that the jury shall be innocent until they can be proved guilty. Members of the jury, you are not here to exchange holiday snapshots. Kindly attend to the proceedings. Try again, my dear. [CZECHOSLOVAKIA *points.*]

No. That is Counsel for the Defence. But you're getting warm. Shall I give you a clue?

CZECHOSLOVAKIA: Please.

[*The* JUDGE *points at* CHAMBERLAIN.]

CZECHOSLOVAKIA: That's him over there. [*She points.*]

JUDGE: Thank you very much, my dear. I trust it won't happen again.

COUNSEL: You have heard the evidence of Czechoslovakia. Do you still have no regrets?

CHAMBERLAIN: I thought Appeasement was the better course.

JUDGE: Mr Witty. If I could interpose. A point that has been puzzling me, and if the jury could drag themselves away from their powder compacts, it would probably be puzzling them too. You are counsel for the defence, are you not?

COUNSEL: I have that honour, m'lud.

JUDGE: And yet as counsel for the defence, you spend your time attacking your client.

COUNSEL: But attack *is* the best form of defence, m'lud.

JUDGE: I underestimated you, Mr Witty.

COUNSEL: My case rests, m'lud.

JUDGE: Good. Good. Now we come to the pith and gist of the proceedings, the sentence. Members of the jury, I want you to consider the following question. Was Mr Neville Chamberlain a mixed blessing. Or was he an unmixed evil. Write on one side of the question only. Neville Joseph Chamberlain, have you anything to say before I pass sentence upon you?

CHAMBERLAIN: I was a very ordinary man, m'lud.

JUDGE: You are not here for offending against the Law of Averages. Anything else?

CHAMBERLAIN: I did die shortly after leaving office.

JUDGE: Mr Chamberlain. It is given to most of us to die at some time or other in our lives. It is no excuse. And keep your mouth shut when you're talking to me. Any extenuating circumstances?

COUNSEL: The accused was born in Birmingham, m'lud.

JUDGE: So are a great many people. It is no excuse.

JUDGE: Prisoner at the Bar. You have been found guilty in the court of history and by full process of time and I have no alternative but to give you a very short sentence, so short indeed that there are only two words in it. Perpetual ignominy.

CHAMBERLAIN: But that sentence is impossible: there's no verb in it.

JUDGE: The verb is understood. Take him down.

Part II

Activities

Growing Up

1 The Graduate

1 In groups, look at the picture below and try to work out what is happening.

2 The picture below depicts the opening scene of a novel, *The Graduate*. In groups, discuss what you think the novel is about.

3 Think about occasions when you have had arguments with your parents. Tell the other members of your group about an argument in which you still think you were right and an argument in which you now realize your parents were right.

4 Read the beginning of *The Graduate* (Growing Up 1), and as you read, try to imagine the scene as the opening of a film.

5 In groups, discuss the following questions:
   a) Benjamin tells his father, 'I have some things on my mind right now.' What do you think these things are?
   b) Why do you think Benjamin refuses to join the party?
   c) Why do you think Benjamin goes for a walk?

6 Imagine that your group is working as a team of scriptwriters and write the film script for the scene when Benjamin returns from his walk and joins the guests at his party.

7 As a group, rehearse and then act out your scene (see 6 above).

8 As a group, a pair or an individual write the last page of the novel, *The Graduate*.

2 No Longer at Ease

1 Think back to your first day at school and then draw a picture of either:
   a) your teacher;
   b) yourself;
   c) a classmate;
   d) the classroom.

2 Form groups. Show each other your drawings and talk about them.

3 As a group, write the opening paragraph of a description of a young boy's or girl's first day in their first job.

4 Combine with another group and read each other your paragraphs. Ask each other questions about what happens to the main characters.

5 You are going to read part of a chapter from a novel which includes the following sentences:
   a) 'Obi's first day in the Civil Service was memorable, almost as memorable as his first day at the bush mission school in Umuofia nearly twenty years before.'
   b) 'Mr Jones was the Inspector of Schools and was feared throughout the province.'
   c) '"Shut up!" roared Mr Jones and followed it with a slap.'
   d) 'That was twenty years ago.'
   e) 'Mr Omo jumped to his feet as soon as Mr Green came in.'
   f) 'He handed it over to Obi with obvious relief. "Mr Okonkwo, for you."'

g) '"You say *sir* to your superior officers, Mr Okonkwo," and the telephone was dropped with a deafening bang.'

Use the sentences above to try to work out where the novel is set and who and what it is about.

6 Read the opening to Chapter Seven of *No Longer at Ease* (Growing Up 2) and as you read, try to work out:
a) why Achebe called the novel 'No Longer at Ease';
b) what Obi did between leaving school and joining the Civil Service;
c) what happens to Obi in the rest of the novel.

7 In groups, talk about your answer to the questions in 6 above.

8 As a group or pair, write a letter either:
a) from Mr Jones to his wife on leave in England;
b) from Mr Green to his wife on leave in England;
c) from Obi to his father.

9 In a group or a pair, write a poem, song, short story or short play about either:
a) the first day at school of a boy or girl in your country, or,
b) the first day at work of a boy or girl in your country.

3 Unreliable Memoirs

1 In groups, tell each other about some of the mischievous things you got involved in as a child.

2 Look at the pictures overleaf. They depict episodes from a book called *Unreliable Memoirs.*
a) In groups, explain what is happening in each picture.
b) Say why you think the book is called 'Unreliable Memoirs'.

3 You are going to read an extract from *Unreliable Memoirs.* In groups, use the pictures to help you to predict what the excerpt will be about.

4 Read the extract from *Unreliable Memoirs* (Growing Up 3) and then, individually, write a descriptive sentence for each of the following:
a) Wally Thorpe
b) Darryl Goodhew
c) Mrs Goodhew
d) Graham Truscott
e) Greg Brennan
f) the author.

5 In groups, look at all the sentences you have written, and write group sentences about each of the characters in 4 above.

Each group should read out its sentences and the class should decide by voting which group has written the most accurate and interesting sentence for each character.

6 In groups:
a) Say what the author's mother meant, when she said, 'I wish your father had come home.'
b) Write the complete rules of 'countries' so that a group who had never heard of the game could play it.

Swap your rules with another group and play the game by following them. Tell the other groups of any defects in their rules and rewrite your own rules if the other groups give you any useful advice.

7 In groups, make up a game called 'Stars', played with a ball, a piece of chalk and a wall.

Write down the rules of the game and then give them to another group for them to play the game.

Play the game given to you by the other group.

8 Write a paragraph about each of the following at the age of twenty-five.
a) Carmel Thorpe
b) Darryl Goodhew
c) Beverley Hindmarsh
d) Warren Hartigan
e) the author.

4 The World According to Garp

1 Think of something very dangerous in your environment and then think how you would warn a young child and an adult stranger about the danger.

2 Form pairs and then pretend your partner is a child and warn him or her about the danger of 1 above.

3 Form different pairs. Pretend your partner is an adult stranger and warn him or her about the danger in 1 above.

4 Form different pairs. Decide on a danger and then:
  a) Write a notice warning people of the danger.
  b) Write a short dialogue in which an adult explains the danger to a young child.

5 Form a group with another pair. Criticize each other's notices and dialogues and then write *one* group warning and *one* group dialogue.

6 You are going to read an extract from a novel in which a small child on a beach is warned about the danger of the undertow (i.e. a strong current in the sea) carrying him out to sea. He mis-hears the word 'undertow' and imagines the danger to be something completely different.

  In groups, discuss what you think the child's imagined danger consists of.

7 Read the extract from *The World According to Garp* (Growing Up 4) and as you read, check your predictions (from 6 above) and try to work out where Garp and Duncan are going and what has happened to Helen and Walt.

8 Either:
  a) Draw a picture of the Under Toad as imagined by Walt. Show your picture to other people and answer questions about why you have drawn it in such a way.

  or

  b) Write a short poem about the Under Toad as though it was written by Walt. Show your poem to other people and answer their questions about it.

9 In groups, discuss the meaning of the last paragraph.

10 In groups, write the next two paragraphs of the novel.

Family

1 The Rain Forest

1 In groups draw up a list of the problems that women face when they are pregnant.

2 Discuss how a man could help his wife to face each of the problems in your list in 1 above.

3 You are going to read an extract from a novel in which a young English wife experiences pregnancy in the tropics. What changes do you think will take place in her life during her pregnancy?

4 Read the extract from *The Rain Forest* (Family 1) and, as you read, try to imagine the daily routine of Kristy's life.

5 In groups answer the following questions:
a) What do you think the Daisy is?
b) Who do you think Ambrose is?
c) What does, 'she was melting into motherhood' mean?
d) Why do you think Kristy's mother wept at the police station?
e) Where do you think the story takes place?
f) Why does Kristy feel sorry for Mrs Axelrod?
Is her pity justified?
g) Why do you think Mrs Axelrod is making a huge circular table-cloth?
Who do you think she is making it for?

6 In groups write a letter from Kristy to:
a) her mother;
b) her best friend in England.

2 The Right True End

1 You are going to read an extract from a novel in which a divorced man responds to a phone call from his brother Chris by driving down the M1 motorway from London to Yorkshire.

In groups, try to predict why he makes the journey and what he thinks about as he is driving.

2 Here are some sentences from the extract. Use them to help you to rethink your predictions from 1 above. The sentences are not in the order they appear in the book.

a) 'I've forgotten, of course, to get back the key.'
b) 'I should at least have asked Chris where they'd taken her so that I could ring up for myself.'
c) 'At least I don't have to wait for trains nowadays, I tell myself as I slip on to the motorway and gently put my foot down.'
d) 'I think if I'd asked her to marry me she'd have stayed.'
e) 'Tenderness, Miriam wanted, tonight of all nights; Miriam who usually grabs sex like a child stuffing its face with chocolates.'
f) 'If anything, my degree and my good job only make her more disappointed that I haven't found another wife and produced a couple of grandchildren to add to Bobby, and Jim's twin girls.'

3 Read the extract from *The Right True End* (Family 2) and as you read, check to see if your predictions were right.

4 In groups, answer the following questions:

a) Why do you think the narrator got divorced from Ingrid?
b) What do you think has happened to him since his divorce?
c) What do you think will happen when he gets to Cressley?
d) What do you think will happen to him when he returns to London?

5 In groups, pairs or individually, do *one* of the following:

a) Write a page from the book describing a scene which takes place on the narrator's return to Cressley.
b) Draw pictures of the narrator, the Old Lady, Ingrid and Miriam.
c) Write a page from a novel set in your country which describes an emergency journey made by a man or women to visit their mother.

3 Billy Liar

1 a) What do you think are the qualities of a good front cover for a paperback book?
  b) Look at the front covers of paperback books that your teacher gives you and judge them against the criteria you have established in a) above.

2 Look at the picture below. It is the front cover for a book called *Billy Liar*. In groups, try to work out in as much detail as you can, what sort of book it is, and what it is about.

3 Swap your conclusions with other groups.

4 In groups, predict how the book will start.

5 Read the beginning of the book (Family 3) and check the passage against your predictions.

6 In the same groups, discuss the accuracy of your predictions and then try to work out what happens next.

7 Now that you know something about the book, judge the quality of the front cover.

8 If you are interested in the book:
 a) Write your version of the next page.
 b) Set an imaginative task related to the book for someone else who is interested in the book.
 c) Do one of the tasks set by a learner in your class.
 d) Borrow the book from the library and as you read it, imagine how you would turn it into a film. (It was made into a film starring Tom Courtenay and Julie Christie.)

4 The Human Factor

1 You are going to read an extract from a novel which includes the following sentences spoken by a character called Mrs Castle.
 a) 'I couldn't help thinking what would have happened to Sam if you and Sarah had been on board.'
 b) 'And then – has it occurred to you, dear, if we are all dead, there might be people – out there – who might claim him?'
 c) 'I'm not at all racialist, though perhaps I'm old-fashioned and patriotic.'
 d) 'He reminds me of you at his age – except for the colour of course.'
 e) 'Since you met Sarah you never mention Mary.
 f) 'Sarah must have *some* relations and they might claim.'

 Read the sentences above carefully, and then in groups, try to answer the following questions:
 a) Who is Mrs Castle talking to?
 b) What is she worried about?
 c) Who is Sam?
 d) Who is Sarah?
 e) Who was Mary?
 f) What do you think Mrs Castle is trying to achieve?

2 Read the extract from *The Human Factor* (Family 4). How many of your answers are right? Discuss each answer with the rest of the group.

3 In groups, read the extract again so that you can answer the following questions:
   a) Who do you think Castle really works for?
   b) How do you think Castle met Sarah?
   c) What do you think is Mrs Castle's attitude to the relationship between Castle and Sarah?
   d) Why do you think Castle has left 'strict directions for Buller to be put away'?
   e) Who was Carson? And why did he die in prison?
   f) Why do you think Sam is a nervous child?
   g) Why do you think Castle is not given a Christian name?
   h) Who do you think are Sam's natural parents?
   i) What do you think happens at the end of the novel?

4 In pairs or groups do *one* of the following:
   a) Write the scene from the novel, in which Castle tells Sarah about his conversation with his mother.
   b) Write a scene from the novel, in which Castle and Sarah discuss what to do in the future.
   c) Write a letter written from abroad by Castle, in which he first tells his mother about his relationship with Sarah.
   d) Write a letter written by Castle to tell Sarah he is in danger and to tell her what to do.

   NB: Show a draft of your work to other pairs or groups and ask them to help you to improve it.

5 In groups, write, rehearse and then act a short scene in which Castle says goodbye to Sarah, to Sam, to Mrs Castle and to Buller, before going overseas on a journey.

5 The Norman Conquests

1 The following extracts are taken from a scene from a play. In groups, look at the statements and work out:
   a) the relationships between the characters;
   b) what happens in the scene.

   (A) Norman: I'll sit here, shall I? All right if I sit here? Anybody any objections if I sit here. (*He is ignored.*) I'll sit here.

   (B) Reg: (*cheerily*) Morning all.

(C) Sarah: (*acid*) Nobody in this house is speaking to you ever again.

(D) Norman: Ha-ha! You spoke to me. Caught you. Caught you.

(E) Annie: Shut up, Norman.

(F) Norman: Ha-ha! Caught you again. That's two of you.

(G) Reg: No, I didn't.

(H) Norman: . . . No Sunday papers. Dear, dear. Ah, well I shall have to read my morning cereal . . . (*He laughs*) Cereal. Do we all get that?

(I) Norman: (*Yelling furiously after her*) I didn't even book the hotel. I knew you wouldn't come. You didn't have the guts.

(J) Norman: The tragedy of my life. Norman Dewers – gigolo and assistant librarian. What's inside you, Reg? Apart from twelve bowls of cornflakes? What do you feel with Sarah?

2 Read the extract from *The Norman Conquests* (Family 5) and check your predictions from 1 above.

3 Form groups of five to act the extract. Choose a director and then decide who will play each of the four characters.

Discuss how you are going to read the play and then rehearse your reading a few times. When you are ready, perform your reading to another group, or record it on cassette or tape.

After listening to another group's reading, compare it to yours and discuss the differences in interpretation.

4 Rewrite the scene as an extract from a novel narrated by either:
a) Annie
b) Sarah
c) Reg
d) Norman
e) an 'uninvolved' narrator.

5 Find two people who have written the scene from different viewpoints from each other and from you.

Read each other's scenes, discuss the differences between them and help each other to improve your first drafts. Then put your scenes together as part of the same chapter of a novel and submit the chapter for assessment by the teacher and/or display it on the wall for people to read.

6 The Ginger Man

1 In groups, list all the causes you can think of for conflict between husband and wife.

2 Read the extract from *The Ginger Man* (Family 6) and try to work out all the reasons for the conflict between Marion and Sebastian.

3 In groups, discuss why you think Marion has decided that she is 'leaving this house'.

4 In groups, write the letter from Sebastian's father to Marion.

5 Do one of the following:
   a) Write a dialogue in which Sebastian talks to a man in a bar about his problems with Marion.
   b) Write a dialogue in which Sebastian tells one of his girlfriends about his problems with Marion.
   c) Rewrite the extract so that it is written in the first person, by Marion.
   d) Write a magazine article in which you campaign against the institution of marriage.

Education

1 Schoolmaster

1 In groups, look at the drawing of a man below and try to work out:
   a) where he is;
   b) who he is;
   c) what he is doing;
   d) what he is thinking about.

2 Share your views with other groups and then as a group, write down what you think might be the details of the man's life.

3 Your teacher is going to read a poem to you about the man in the drawing. Take another good look at the drawing and then close your eyes and picture the man and the room he is in. As your teacher reads the poem look carefully at the man and at what he is doing.

4 Think about the following questions and then be prepared to answer them in class discussion.
   a) Why was the teacher sad?
   b) What do you feel towards him?
   c) What do his pupils feel towards him?
   d) Where do you think his wife has gone?
   e) Why do you think his wife has left him?
   f) Why do you think he talks to his 'auntie'?

5 Read the poem 'Schoolmaster' (Education 1).

6 Do *one* of the following activities:
   a) Practise reading the poem aloud so as to achieve dramatic effect.
   b) Paint or draw your interpretation of the poem.
   c) Write the teacher's diary for the week in which his wife left him.
   d) Write a letter from the teacher's wife explaining why she has decided to leave him.
   e) Write a short story version of the poem through the eyes of the teacher.
   f) Turn the poem into the beginning of a play and practise acting it out.
   g) Write one of the following:
      an extra verse for the poem;
      a first language version of the poem;
      a poem beginning:
         'The window gives onto the green tree . . .'.

   NB: You can do your activity individually, in a pair, or as a member of a group.

7 If you want to, present your activity to the class (e.g. read the poem aloud, display and explain your picture, read your short story aloud, act your play, etc.)

2 The Chip-Chip Gatherers

1 In groups, discuss what you think should be the main objectives of secondary-school education.

   List your objectives in order of importance and then compare them with those of other groups.

2 You are going to read an extract from a novel which describes a boy's education in Port-of-Spain, Trinidad. It includes the following excerpts:

a) '– especially add and subtract because that is what your life will be about.'
b) '. . . Wilbert neglected the frills of education . . .'
c) 'These accomplishments successfully achieved, the education of Wilbert Ramsaran came to an effective end.'
d) 'His teachers complained to Egbert Ramsaran.'
e) 'That is all I send him to school to learn in the first place.'

In groups, say why you think Wilbert's father sent him to school and what he hoped Wilbert would have achieved by the time he left school.

3 Read the extract from *The Chip-Chip Gatherers* (Education 2) and check your predictions (from 2 above).

4 In groups, write Wilbert's school report for his final term at school.

5 Write a magazine article entitled, 'Should Teachers Give Parents What They Want?'

6 Write a scene from a novel in which a middle-aged Wilbert is telling one of his sons why he wants him to go to university.

3 Unreliable Memoirs

1 In groups, talk about your memories of your first day at school. Describe people, things and events which you can remember, and mention things which you realize that you cannot remember at all.

2 Draw one of your primary-school teachers you had strong feelings about. Then on separate sheets of paper:
a) Describe your feelings for the teacher.
b) Write a quotation (remembered or made up) from the teacher addressing the class.
NB: Use different pens or pencils for each activity, and print your descriptions and quotations.

3 In groups, place all your drawings face down on one pile, all your descriptions face down on another pile and all your quotations on a third pile.

Shuffle the piles and then put the pieces of paper face up on a desk.

Move to another group's desk and match their drawings, descriptions and quotations. Then join together with the other group to check the success of your matchings.

4 Read the extract from *Unreliable Memoirs* (Education 3) and as you read, draw Miss Turnbull talking to the author when he was in her class.

Compare your drawings with those of the other members of your group and discuss their similarities and differences.

5 In groups, write descriptions of the author:
a) as a small boy;
b) as an adult.

6 Write an extract from your own autobiography in which you list childhood incidents that you can remember, and speculate on their effect on your life. Try to make your extract amusing.

Give your extract to members of your group and, later, discuss their reactions to it.

4 The Natural Order

1 Imagine that you are a young teacher about to start your teaching career in the school below:

a) The night before your first day in the school, you are preparing your first lesson with 3B, a troublesome class of fourteen-year-old boys whose class teacher has just left the school in the middle of the term. Use the following framework to help you to make notes in preparation for your lesson.

CLASS 3B	LESSON – ENGLISH LITERATURE
Aims:	
Stages of the Lesson:	
Possible Problems:	Solutions:

b) In groups, form, compare and discuss your notes and then write group notes.
c) Present your group notes to the class or another group, and ask them for their reaction.
d) In your group, discuss whether or not you intend to use corporal punishment to help you to maintain discipline.

2 Read the extract from *The Natural Order* (Education 4) and as you read, try to visualize the scenes in the school, through the eyes of Miss Slade.

3 As a class, give answers to the following questions:
a) What were Miss Slade's main problems?
b) Who was to blame for these problems?
c) What could Miss Slade have done to prevent some of the problems?
d) What could Miss Slade have done to deal more effectively with the problems that faced her?
e) What do you think will happen to Miss Slade at the school?

4 In groups, answer the following questions:
a) What was Martin's 'small disappointment'?
b) What did Martin mean by saying, 'Punishment is swift and painful'?

c) What did Martin really mean when he said, 'I expect you to give her all the co-operation and respect you had for Mr Fallowfield.'
d) What did Miss Slade mean when she thought, 'Surely I did not have to teach them as well?'
e) Why were Miss Slade's words inappropriate when she said, 'Can you please summarize your curriculum under Mr Fallowfield'?

5 Which of the following words and phrases could be used to describe Martin, which could be used to describe Miss Slade and which could *not* be used to describe either?

a martinet
a disciplinarian
a hypocrite
a pacifist
timorous
optimistic
obliging
boorish
naïve
cantankerous
humane
cynical
ineffectual
ill-prepared

In groups, complete the following table:

Words describing Martin	Reasons
Words describing Miss Slade	Reasons
Words not describing either	Reasons

6 In pairs, write short dialogues for *two* of the following situations:
a) Martin talking to Miss Slade after the lesson;
b) Miss Slade talking to Riccio after the end of the lesson;
c) Miss Slade phoning her mother after her first day at the school;
d) Riccio telling a friend in another class about the new teacher;
e) The Headmaster giving Miss Slade some friendly advice.

When you have finished, ask another pair to join you and then criticize each other's dialogues and make suggestions for making them more appropriate, accurate and effective. Then rewrite your dialogues and either hand them to the teacher for marking, or display them for other pairs to read and comment on.

7 Either:
a) Write a letter from Miss Slade to her best friend describing her first two days at the school.
or
b) Form a group and devise the opening scene of a play about a new teacher starting work in a school in your country (or in any country other than England). Rehearse your scene and then, if you want to, perform it for the class.
NB: Try to make your scene realistic and amusing and to use it to reflect your experience and criticisms of *education.*

5 The Malayan Trilogy

1 Read the following extract from a letter and answer these questions as you read it.
a) Who wrote the letter?
b) Who was it written to?
c) Think of reasons why the letter was written.

Dear Sir,
I hope you will forgive my writing to you like this, but I find that I am becoming increasingly disturbed by some of the things that Mr Crabbe, the History Master, is saying in class, especially about the running of the School. I know I speak for all the boys when I say that he should not say these things. He is speaking as though he should be running the School himself and is always criticizing the things that you, sir, do to make the School an efficient and happy School.
First he said the expulsion of Hamidin was wrong. Then he said it was wrong to cane prefects when they have done wrong. Then he said it was not right to deprive the School of a holiday when, as is well known, it was the only way to make the School realize that they must do better work in the examinations. Then he said that you, sir, did not listen fairly to the things the boys say when they come to see you. Also, I believe that Mr Crabbe has many wrong political ideas and talks about freedom and independence when he really means communism.
One day he called me into his flat and asked me many questions. He seemed annoyed that I was trying to help the younger boys to see how wrong Communism is. He said to me as follows . . .

2 You are going to read an extract from a novel which includes the letter you have just read above. In this extract Mr Crabbe is told:

a) '. . . you'd made up your mind to be away. You knew what was going to happen.'
b) 'You know damn well what happened. Nothing happened.'
c) 'All I know is that it was your idea.'
d) 'Ever since you've been here you've been encouraging the boys to go against discipline.'
e) 'You made me and everybody look a pack of fools.'
f) 'I'll tell you what's going to happen to you, Crabbe. You're being transferred, and with a bloody bad report, too.'

In groups, try to predict:

a) who is talking to Crabbe;
b) where the discussion is taking place;
c) why the person who is talking to Crabbe is so angry;
d) what exactly has happened in Crabbe's absence.

When you have finished, compare your predictions with those of other groups.

3 Read the extract from *The Malayan Trilogy* (Education 5) and, as you read, check to see if your predictions were correct.

4 In groups, try to work out what happened, who caused it to happen and why.

Compare your decisions with those of other groups.

5 Divide into four groups. Group 1 should prepare themselves as Crabbe, about to be questioned by the Chief Inspector of Schools. They should talk about the questions they expect to be asked and should decide how to answer the questions.

Group 2 should prepare themselves as Boothby, and should talk about what they are likely to be asked and what they will say.

Group 3 should prepare themselves as the Chinese prefect, and should work out what to say when they are questioned.

Group 4 should prepare themselves as the Chief Inspector of Schools, and should work out what questions to ask Boothby, Crabbe and the Chinese prefect.

6 Form groups of four so that in each group there is one person from Group 1, one from Group 2, one from Group 3 and one from Group 4 (i.e. one Crabbe, one Boothby, one Chinese prefect and one Chief Inspector of Schools).

Act out a meeting in which the Chief Inspector of Schools questions Boothby, Crabbe and the Chinese prefect about the events on Sports Day and the accusations against Crabbe.

7 Imagine that you are the Chief Inspector of Schools and write a report on your visit to Boothby's school.

Love

Introduction

1 Look at the drawing below and then in groups discuss what it says to you about love.

Picasso, 'The Lovers'

2 Find and discuss other drawings, pictures, photos, etc. depicting love, and then compile a list of different types of love.

Compare your list with those of other groups.

1 Efuru

1 In groups find out the meanings of the following:
a) a dowry
b) an arranged marriage
c) courting
d) bride price

e) customs
f) engagement
g) fiancé
h) ceremony

2 In groups make generalizations about the differences in engagement and marriage customs in different parts of the world.

3 In groups discuss the following statements:
a) 'A man and a woman who are in love should live together and not worry about such old-fashioned customs as marriage.'
b) 'No couple should be allowed to marry unless both sets of parents give their blessing.'
c) 'Marriages arranged by parents are often the most happy.'

4 Read the extract from *Efuru* (Love 1) and as you read, think about Efuru's actions and decide whether each one of them was wise.

5 In groups discuss the following statements:
a) Efuru was stupid to agree to marry a man who she had only been courting for two weeks.
b) Efuru was stupid to agree to marry a man who could not afford her dowry.
c) Efuru should have told her father that she was going to live with Adizua.
d) Adizua's mother should not have allowed Efuru to join their household.
e) Efuru's father should have gone to see her himself instead of sending young men from the village.
f) The young men should have taken Efuru back to her father instead of accepting Efuru's hospitality.
g) Efuru behaves in an independent way which all women in all societies should be allowed to behave in.

6 In groups turn the extract into a scene from a play and practise acting it.

Perform your scene for the class and then help to decide which group's play is the most interesting and the best acted.

7 In groups predict what will happen after the young men have returned to their village, and then write the next page of the novel.

2 How Far Can You Go?

1 In groups, discuss the difference between:

love	a crush	worship
infatuation	lust	friendship
passion	affection	affinity

Give examples to illustrate your distinctions (from books, films, plays, real life, etc.) and then share your discussion with the teacher and with the rest of the class.

2 You are going to read an extract from a novel in which a secretary called Lynn has a crush on her boss, a married man called Dennis. The extract takes place during the Christmas Party at the factory where Lynn and Dennis work.

In groups, predict what happens at the party and then practise miming the scene. Each group should mime their scene to another group and then invite that group to tell their story.

3 The extract you are going to read contains the following:

A project was forming in his head
he realized he had been wanting to do for some time
'You know, I could really fancy you Dennis,' said Doreen
'Anyway, I think she's gone home.'
'I was just leaving you a card.'
'You've got lipstick all over your face.'
'I can't wait that long,'
and drew her into his arms
Dennis's feeble lust
'Shall I take you home?'
'Can we try and forget this ever happened?'

In your groups, revise your predictions about what happens in the extract.

4 Read the extract from *How Far Can You Go?* (Love 2) and check your predictions.

5 In groups, write:
a) the next 20 lines of the novel;
b) the first five lines of each of the remaining chapters in the novel;
c) the last 10 lines of the novel.

3 The Heart of the Matter

1 In groups, discuss how you would go about working out the setting of a novel from an analysis of an extract from it. What clues would you look for?

2 In groups, read the extract from *The Heart of the Matter* (Love 3) and try to work out where it is set. You do not have to read it all silently and then discuss the task; talk about it as you find clues in the text.

3 Share your conclusions with other groups or with the whole class.

4 Form different groups and work out:
a) when the novel takes place;
b) who the characters are and what the relationships between them are;
c) what has happened in the book before this scene.

5 Share your conclusions with the class.

6 In the same groups, write the next page of the novel.

7 If you are interested in the book, ask your teacher for its title and read it. As you read, compare your deductions with what happens in the text and compare your group's page with the equivalent one in the novel.

4 Sentence of Death

1 You are going to read a short story called *The Sentence of Death.* What do you think it is going to be about? Look at the picture opposite.

2 In groups, predict the story from the title, from the drawing, and from the first sentence and last sentence of the story, below.

> There was this bloke sitting at his bench at work one day when he came all over funny, so he got up and went to see the works doctor, who examined him thoroughly.
>
> 'Oh aye,' she said. 'It's all right for you, but I've got to get up in the morning.'

3 Read the story (Love 4) and as you read, try to predict what is coming next.

4 In groups, answer the questions below:
a) Why do you think Mr Murphy is given the afternoon off?
b) Why is Mrs Murphy upset by her husband's news?
c) What did Mrs Murphy mean when she said, 'you've still got one and three-quarter hours to kill.'?
d) Why do you think Mrs Murphy refuses her husband's last request?
e) What does the story tell us about the marriage between Mr and Mrs Murphy?
f) Why do you think Terry Morgan wrote this particular story?

5 In groups, write an epitaph to go on Mr Murphy's grave. Try to make the epitaph funny and to summarize Mr Murphy's life, marriage and death.

Read the other groups' epitaphs and help to decide which is the funniest and most apt.

6 In groups, rewrite the story so that it is Mrs Murphy who is told that she only has four hours to live.

5 My Name Blew Like a Horn Among the Payira

1 You are going to listen to your teacher reading part of a poem called 'Song of Lawino'. In this poem a Ugandan wife complains about the treatment she gets from her husband.

Before you listen to the poem, form groups and note down:
a) what you think a wife in your country might complain about;
b) what you expect the Ugandan wife to complain about.

2 Listen to your teacher reading an extract from 'Song of Lawino' and as you listen, try to imagine what Lawino and Ocol look like, and to decide whether Lawino's complaints are justified.

3 In groups, answer the following questions:
a) What does Lawino complain about?
b) Do you think her complaints are justified?
c) Why do you think Ocol treats Lawino as he does?
d) What problems of Third World countries are illustrated in the poem?

4 Read the extract from 'Song of Lawino' (Love 5) and as you read, check your answers to 1b) and 3 above.

5 Choose *one* of the following activities and then work individually, in pairs or in groups, as appropriate.
a) Mime the poem as it is read aloud by one of the group.
b) Draw a series of pictures to illustrate the poem.
c) Write a short extract from the 'Song of Ocol'.
d) Write a scene from a play about Lawino and Ocol.
e) Write a poem or story about yourself in which you complain about aspects of your present condition and look back to a time when things seemed better.

When you have finished, get an individual, a pair or a group to look at what you have produced and to help you to make it better.

Society

1 The Happy Haven

1 In groups, discuss the following statements:
   a) Old people should be looked after by their children.
   b) Old people should never be allowed to be lonely.
   c) The government should look after old people by providing them with free places in old people's homes.
   d) Old people should be helped by their families and their government to remain independent and to look after themselves.
   e) Governments should not waste money keeping old people alive in loneliness and misery.

2 In groups, tell each other about an old person who you admire or who you feel sorry for.

3 Your teacher is going to read you a poem spoken by an old lady. Look at the photographs of three old ladies below and as you listen to the poem, decide which old lady you think the poem is about.

4 Discuss with your neighbour your reaction to the old lady in the poem and answer the following questions:
 a) Do you like the lady? Why?
 b) What three words would you use to describe the lady?
 c) If the lady was your mother how would you feel?
 d) Which photograph do you think is of the lady in the poem? Why?

 Share your views with the teacher and the rest of the class.

5 Read the extract from 'The Happy Haven' (Society 1) that you have just listened to.

6 As an individual, in a pair or in a group do *one* of the following:
 a) Paint or draw a picture to illustrate the poem.
 b) Write this week's entry in the old lady's diary.
 c) Write a letter from the old lady to her son in Australia.
 d) Accept the old lady's invitation, 'That's me. Now: you', and write a poem about either:
 yourself;
 yourself as the child of the old lady;
 yourself as an old man or woman.

7 Form groups of four and in each group give each member of the group one of the following roles:
 a) the old lady's son;
 b) the old lady's daughter-in-law;
 c) the old lady's grandson;
 d) the old lady's younger brother.

 Hold a family meeting and make decisions about what you are going to do to help the old lady.

 Share your decisions with the teacher and with other groups.

2 The Rabbits Who Caused All the Trouble

1 a) In groups, tell each other about any animal fables you can remember from your own country.
 b) Talk about the different reasons why people write or tell animal fables.

2 You are going to read an animal fable. Look at the clues below and then, in groups, predict what the story is going to be about.

a) *Title:*

The Rabbits Who Caused All the Trouble.

b) *First Two Sentences:*

Within the memory of the youngest child there was a family of rabbits who lived near a pack of wolves. The wolves announced that they did not like the way the rabbits were living.

c) *Last Two Sentences:*

So the wolves gave them one. 'They were trying to escape,' said the wolves, 'and, as you know, this is no world for escapists.'

d) *Illustration*

Look at the drawing below.

e) *Moral*

Run, don't walk, to the nearest desert island.

3 Read 'The Rabbits who Caused All The Trouble' (Society 2). As you read, check your predictions.

4 In groups, answer the following questions:
a) Who do the wolves represent?
b) Who do the rabbits represent?

c) Who was to blame for what happened to the rabbits?
d) List and explain any examples of irony you can find in the story.
e) List and explain any puns you can find in the story.
f) What do you think Thurber hoped to achieve in writing this story?
g) Think of a real modern day or historical event which is similar to the one described in the story.

5 In groups, write a similar animal fable about *one* of the following:
a) greed
b) selfishness
c) miserliness.

3 The Interpreters

1 Think about (or make up) an incident in your life which caused you embarrassment. Imagine that you are going to write a story about the incident, and write the first sentence of your story.

2 In groups, look at the first sentences of your group members' stories and try to guess what happens in their stories.

3 Tell each other about your embarrassing incidents.

4 You are going to read about incidents which cause embarrassment to Faseyi. Look at the following information about the incident and then in groups write notes about what you think happens.
a) The incidents take place at a cocktail party given by an ambassador in Nigeria.
b) Faseyi is a 'westernized' Nigerian who is very concerned about appearances.
c) Faseyi's wife, Monica, is not concerned about appearances.
d) One of the incidents involves the drinking of palm wine, a cheap and delicious drink obtained by tapping palm trees.

5 In groups, read the extract from *The Interpreters* (Society 3) and as you read, check your predictions. Instead of reading the whole passage silently and then discussing it, talk to each other as you read.

6 In groups, discuss your reactions to the following statements:
a) The ambassador was making fun of Monica.
b) Bandele got the steward to bring Monica a glass of palm wine in order to embarrass Faseyi.
c) Monica had decided to embarrass Faseyi before she went to the party.
d) Monica is not a Nigerian.

e) Bandele tries to help Faseyi but Kola deliberately tries to make the situation worse for him.
f) Monica is improperly dressed for a formal function.
g) Monica is right not to worry about appearances.

7 In groups, either:
a) Write the next two paragraphs of the novel.
b) Devise and act out a scene in your country during which one of the characters causes social embarrassment.

4 Close Encounters of the Third Kind

1 Anyone who has seen the film *Close Encounters of the Third Kind* should try to summarize the film for the class or a group and in particular should try to describe in detail the scene in which the spaceship lands.

Students who have not seen the film should ask questions, to make sure they get a clear picture of what it is about.

2 Read the passage (Society 4), then discuss in groups any differences between the book and the film.

3 Either:
a) In groups, paint the 'great ship' as it is described in the book.

When you have finished, discuss your paintings with other groups.

or

b) Rewrite the extract as though it was written by one of the people in the ship.

4 In groups, devise, rehearse and perform a radio dramatization of the scene.

5 In groups, write, rehearse and perform the debriefing scene as part of a radio play.

5 Midnight's Children

1 The class divides into two halves, A and B.

2 Form groups of five (if possible) within A and B.

3 a) Groups in A make up an incident which is ludicrous because one of the characters insists on sticking rigidly to a code of behaviour which is not appropriate to the situation.

Each group practises miming their story and when they are ready they mime their story to another group in A and get them to tell the story.

b) Groups in B read the extract from *Midnight's Children* (Society 5) and then practise miming the incident in the extract. Try to mime it so that people who have not read the extract will be able to work out exactly what happens.

4 Each group in A should join with a group in B. The A group should mime their story and get the B group to tell them the story. The A group then tells them if they are right.

The B group then mimes the extract from *Midnight's Children* to the A group and asks the A group to tell the story. The B group does not tell the A group if they are right.

5 The A groups read the extract from *Midnight's Children* to check to see if their version of the story is correct.

The students in the B groups read the extract again to try to predict what happens on each of the next three visits that Doctor Aziz makes to Ghani's house.

6 a) Each member of an A group forms a pair by joining a member of a B group.

Each pair notes down what they think happens on each of Doctor Aziz's next three visits to Ghani's house.

b) Each pair joins with another pair and they compare and explain their predictions.

7 Each pair writes *one* of the following:

a) a description of Doctor Aziz's fourth visit to Ghani's house;

or

b) a short story of their own describing a ridiculous incident caused by someone sticking rigidly to an inappropriate code of behaviour.

6 The Public Image

1 You are going to read an extract from a novel called *The Public Image*.

In groups answer the following questions:

a) What is a public image?

b) What sort of people have a public image?
c) Who creates public images?
d) Why are public images created?
e) What damage can public images do?

2 In the extract you are going to read a film star's husband has written letters to his girlfriend about his wife and has then committed suicide. What advice do you think the film star is given by her producer?

3 Read the extract from *The Public Image* (Society 6) and as you read, try to work out why Frederick has committed suicide and why Luigi gives Annabel the advice that he does.

4 In groups answer the following questions:
a) How did Frederick die?
b) Why did Annabel go to the hospital?
c) Who is Billy O'Brien?
d) Who is Marina?
e) What do you think Frederick wrote in his letters to Marina?
f) What sacrifices do you think Annabel has made to become and remain a film star?
g) Why would the publication of the letters have finished Annabel's film career?

5 In groups imagine that you are journalists working for a particular newspaper in England or America and write an article on Frederick's suicide and inquest.

6 Imagine that it is now two years since Frederick's death and that Billy is hard up and has decided to sell 'the truth' about Frederick's suicide to a newspaper. Write the newspaper article which discloses the truth.

7 Write the last paragraph of the novel, *The Public Image*.

7 Indecent Exposure

1 You are going to read an extract from a novel. In groups, use the following clues to help you to predict the type and content of the novel.

Title

Indecent Exposure

Illustration

Look at the part of the front cover shown overleaf.

Reviews

'The brilliant follow-up to *Riotous Assembly* . . .'
'Explosively funny, fiendishly inventive'
(*The Sunday Times*)
'A lusty and delightfully lunatic fantasy'
(*Sunday Express*)
'All good, dirty fun'
(*The Daily Telegraph*)

Sample Sentences

'It was Heroes Day in Piemburg and as usual the little capital of Zululand was quite unwarrantably gay.'
'Only the Zulus were forbidden to commemorate the occasion. . . .'
'"Nothing to worry about," he said. "It's stuffed."'
'"Congratulations on winning this award . . ."'
'"With his bare hands," said the Kommandant.'

2 Read the extract from *Indecent Exposure* (Society 7) and as you read, think about the author's satirical targets.

3 The class divides into two halves, A and B. Those students in A form groups and prepare themselves to be Tom Sharpe, being interviewed about *Indecent Exposure*. Read the extract again and anticipate and prepare for questions you think might be asked during the interview.

Those students in B form groups and prepare themselves to be journalists interviewing Tom Sharpe about *Indecent Exposure*. Write the questions you are going to ask.

4 Form pairs with a student from A and a student from B in each. Act out the interview between the journalist and Tom Sharpe.

5 In groups, decide whether each of the following statements is true or false and be prepared to give reasons for your decisions.

a) Kommandant Van Heerden was an Afrikaner who believed in reconciliation between the Afrikaners and the British, and in racial harmony.

b) Konstabel Els was an extremely brave policeman and staunch Christian, who had died on duty.

c) Konstabel Els had killed a lot of black men, had slept with a lot of black women and had killed a Dobermann Pincher with his bare hands.

d) The police force of Piemburg followed an unofficial policy of cruel discrimination against blacks.

e) Konstabel von Rooyen won the Els Memorial Trophy for the action he took to prevent a prisoner from trying to escape.

f) Luitenant Verkramp was interested in the use of electro-convulsive therapy because he was attracted to Dr von Blimenstein and because he was interested in using it to help to cure prisoners who were suffering from manic depression.

When you have finished, share your views with another group and/or the whole class.

8 The World According to Garp

1 a) In groups, discuss the Women's Liberation Movement and in particular talk about:
the reasons for its development;
its objectives;
its achievements in your country and throughout the world.

b) As an individual, write two or three sentences summarizing your own personal attitude towards Women's Liberation.

Show your sentences to other students and defend them, if you are challenged.

2 Read the extract from *The World According to Garp* (Society 8) and as

you read, try to answer the following questions:
a) Why is Garp dressed in women's clothes?
b) What was the relationship between Garp and Jenny Fields?
c) Who was Roberta Muldoon and who is she now?
d) What is the meeting at the School of Nursing for?

3 In groups, answer the questions in 2 above.

4 In groups, discuss what points you think are being raised about the Women's Movement by the author of the extract you have just read.

Write down the implicit questions that you think the author is asking the reader and also write down your group answers.

Compare your questions and answers with those of other groups.

5 In groups write a short article on the Ellen Jamesians for each of the following:
a) a magazine dedicated to the Women's Movement;
b) a men's magazine;
c) a newspaper which prides itself on being objective.

9 Telephone Conversation

1 You are going to read a poem about a Nigerian in England who is phoning a landlady to try to rent himself a flat.

What problems do you think he might experience during the conversation?

Look at the beginning of the poem and in groups try to put in the missing words.

> The ______ seemed reasonable, location
> Indifferent. The landlady swore she ______
> Off premises. Nothing remained
> But self-confession. 'Madam,' I ______,
> 'I hate a ______ journey – I am ______.'

What do you think the landlady's reaction will be to the man's announcement?

Do you think he will get the flat?

2 Read the poem, 'Telephone Conversation' (Society 9), and as you read, try to picture the man and the woman on opposite ends of the phone.

3 In groups:
   a) Discuss your immediate reaction to the poem and what it is trying to say.
   b) Draw a picture to illustrate the poem, and then join together with another group and discuss both of your pictures and the interpretations of the poem that they represent.
   c) Comment on each of the following statements about the man in the poem:
      (1) He was unnecessarily rude to the woman.
      (2) He had probably made many similar phone calls.
      (3) He succeeded in humiliating the woman whilst appearing to be polite.
      (4) He should not have told the woman he was African.
      (5) He should have put the phone down as soon as the woman asked him, 'How dark?'
   d) Explain why the man said 'You mean – like plain or milk chocolate?'
   e) Say what you think is the significance of the man's question:
      '. . . wouldn't you rather
      See for yourself?'

4 In pairs or groups do one of the following:
   a) Rewrite the poem as the beginning of a short story and add a scene in which the man meets the landlady.
   b) Write a poem about yourselves arriving in a strange country.
   c) Write the beginning of a novel or a play about someone arriving in a strange country.

5 As an individual, imagine you are Wole Soyinka and write a short letter about your arrival in England to:
   a) your parents;
   b) a close friend in Nigeria.

Sport

1 The Greatest

1 You are going to read extracts from a book called *The Greatest*. In groups, predict who and what it might be about.

2 One of the extracts begins, 'Louisville 100 miles. I barely see the sign in the rain', and the other begins, 'The crowd eggs me on: 'ALI! ALI! BOMAYE!' One of the extracts includes the sentence, 'You finished, loud-mouth! You finished!' and the other includes the sentence, 'The referee raises my hand in victory.'

Think about your group predictions in 1 above and decide whether you want to modify them before reading the extract.

3 Form pairs, and in each pair let one person be A and the other B. A should read extract A from *The Greatest* (Sport 1) and B should read extract B from the same book (following extract A).

When you have finished reading, A should tell B about his or her extract and B should tell A about his or her extract.

4 Work together in your pair to answer the following questions, without looking at the extracts:

a) Why do you think these two particular extracts from *The Greatest* have been selected and presented together?
b) Who does Angelo Dundee call 'Savages'?
c) Why does he call them savages?
d) What is ironic about these particular people being called savages?
e) Why do the crowd celebrate Ali's victory over George Foreman and why do the crowd taunt Ali so much when he loses to Ken Norton?
f) What do you learn about Ali's personality from the two extracts?

5 As a pair, read both of the two extracts to check your answers to a) – f) in 4 above. Whenever you find some evidence, stop and discuss it in relation to your answers.

6 Revise your answers to a) – f); join with another pair and compare your answers.

7 As a group of four, choose or invent a famous sports star, filmstar or politician and map out an outline of a chapter from his or her autobiography, describing either the worst or greatest day in their career.

As a group, write one page of the autobiography from either the chapter describing the worst day or the chapter describing the greatest day.

8 Pass your page on to another group and take their page from them. Read their page and then write the page from their autobiography which describes the opposite of the page they gave you (e.g. describe the worst day in his or her career if they give you a page describing his or her greatest day).

2 Journey to Wembley

1 In groups, find out where and what Wembley is, and try to work out what a book called *Journey to Wembley* might be about.

2 You are going to read an extract from the book which describes the scene in the Liverpool dressing room after a Cup Final against Manchester United.

In pairs, try to answer the following questions as quickly as you can, by reading extract A from *Journey to Wembley* (Sport 2). See if you can be the first pair to find the answers to all the questions:

a) What was the score in the match?
b) Who scored for Liverpool?
c) Who scored the winning goal?
d) What do you think might be meant by the Double?
e) Who was the manager of Liverpool?
f) Which team lost in the Cup Final the previous year?
g) Which team were due to play in the European Cup Final in the following week?
h) What was the 'journey' referred to in the book?

3 Take part in a class discussion of the answers to the questions in 2 above.

4 Read the extract again and try to imagine how each player mentioned really feels.

5 In pairs, write the Cup Final Day diary entry for two of the following:
  a) Clemence
  b) Keegan
  c) Smith
  d) Hughes
  e) Kennedy
  f) McDermott
  g) Paisley.

6 As an individual, write two paragraphs of the autobiography of Emlyn Hughes in which you describe the scene in the Liverpool dressing room after the Cup Final.

7 Extract B describes the scenes after Liverpool had played in the European Cup Final in Italy the Wednesday after losing the Cup Final to Manchester United.

  In pairs, try to imagine the scene and to predict what the extract describes.

8 Read extract B and see if your predictions were right.

9 Write a brief report (about 150 words) of the scene in the Liverpool dressing room in Italy, for an English newspaper.

3 Looks and Smiles

1 In groups, discuss your reactions to the following statements:
  a) If you love someone you should try to share their enthusiasms.
  b) If you love someone you should not expect them to always share your enthusiasms.
  c) It is not a good idea for people who are in love to always do everything together.
  d) It is not a good idea for a boy to take his girlfriend to a football match with him.
  e) Ultimately, friendships with other men are more important to most men than love affairs with women.
  f) If you support a sports team, all that really matters is that they win.
  g) It is very selfish to expect a friend or lover to give up something they are really interested in.

2 Read the extract from *Looks and Smiles* (Sport 3) and decide whether you sympathize with Mick or with Karen.

3 In groups, discuss whether you sympathize with Mick or with Karen.

4 In groups, answer the following questions:
  a) Why do you think Mick took Karen to the match?
  b) Why do you think Karen agreed to go to the match with Mick?
  c) Why did Mick not want his mates to know he was taking Karen to the match?
  d) How often do you think Karen had been to a football match before? Why?
  e) Was Mick justified in being annoyed with Karen?
  f) Was Karen right in describing Mick as 'horrible'?

5 In groups, complete the final paragraph.

6 In groups, decide what you think Mick should do when he is accused by Karen of being horrible.

7 As individuals, write the next page of the novel.

4 Professional Foul

1 The following utterances are made by a character called McKendrick in a play called *Professional Foul*. In groups, look at them carefully and decide:
  a) what McKendrick is talking about;
  b) what McKendrick's views are;
  c) what your own views are on the points that McKendrick makes.

(i) I'm a professional philosopher. You'll do well to listen to what I have to say.

(ii) How can you expect the kids to be little gentlemen when their heroes behave like yobs?

(iii) Roy here is sensitive because he gave away a penalty today, by a deliberate foul. To stop a certain goal he hacked a chap down. After all, a penalty might be saved and broken legs are quite rare – (BROADBENT *stands up but* MCKENDRICK *pacifies him with a gesture.*)
It's perfectly all right – you were adopting the utilitarian values of the game, for the good of the team, for England! But I'm not talking about particular acts of expediency. No, I'm talking about the whole *ethos*.

(iv) I can't remember one occasion in all those years and *years* when the player who touched the ball last didn't realize it. So, what I want to know *is* – why is it that on Match of the Day, every time the bloody ball goes into touch, both players claim the throw-in for their own side? I merely ask for information. Is it because they are very, very stupid or is it because a dishonest advantage is as welcome as an honest one?

(v) Here's a question for anthropologists. Name me a tribe which organizes itself into teams for sporting encounters and greets every score against their opponents with paroxysms of childish glee, whooping, dancing and embracing in an ecstasy of crowing self-congratulation in the very midst of their disconsolate fellows? – Who are these primitives who pile all their responses into the immediate sensation, unaware or uncaring of the long undulations of life's fortunes?

2 In groups, try to predict:
   a) who McKendrick is;
   b) where McKendrick is;
   c) who McKendrick is talking to;
   d) what has just taken place.

3 Read the extract from *Professional Foul* (Sport 4) and as you read, decide what your reactions are to each of the characters you meet.

4 In groups, comment on the following statements:
   a) McKendrick is being aggressive because he is drunk and because he is a failure in his own field.
   b) Broadbent proves that footballers are yobs by punching McKendrick.
   c) McKendrick proves by his comments that he does not really know anything about sport.
   d) McKendrick is foolish to philosophize so much about sport, as sport is about action and excitement and not about thought.
   e) McKendrick is right when he attacks the ethos which encourages people to foul in order to win.

5 In groups, answer the following questions:
   a) What does McKendrick mean by 'the utilitarian values of the game'?
   b) What do you think McKendrick is referring to when he says, 'Sorry about that business in the lift, by the way, Tommy.'
   c) What does McKendrick mean when he says, 'Tomorrow in my experience is usually the same day'?
   d) What does McKendrick mean when he describes Anderson as 'one of life's cricketers'?
   e) What does McKendrick mean by referring to himself as 'the Roy Broadbent of Stoke'?

6 Imagine that you are McKendrick and that you are making notes as a preparation for writing your autobiography. In groups, note down the important details of your upbringing, education, career and private life.

Conflict

Introduction

In groups look at the picture below and discuss your reaction to it.

Picasso, 'Guernica'

In particular, discuss what you think the artist was trying to say in this painting and what the painting actually says to you.

1 The Birthday Party

1 You are going to read an extract from a play called *The Birthday Party*. In groups, list the possible locations, themes and characters for this play.

2 Read the extract from *The Birthday Party* (Confict 1) and as you read, try to work out McCann's motives for attending Stanley's birthday party.

3 Read the extract again and then close your eyes and act out the scene in your head. Try to visualize the scene and the characters in detail and to give each character an individual voice and interpretation.

4 In groups decide which of the following adjectives are valid as descriptions of the characters.

a) *Stanley*

mild	frightened	gregarious
aggressive	inquisitive	lonely
nervous	resolute	trusting
guilty	apprehensive	puzzled

b) *McCann*

aggressive	amiable	intimidating
sociable	considerate	devious
menacing	sinister	mocking
sarcastic	nervous	hostile

5 In pairs read the scene aloud with the following different interpretations:

a) Stanley – nervous; frightened; guilty conscience.
McCann – menacing; controlled anger; seeking revenge.

b) Stanley – aggressive; unsociable; drunk.
McCann – polite; amiable.

c) Any other intepretation you can think of.

6 In groups, write and then act the next page of the play.

2 A Visit from the Footbinder

1 Think about all the issues that men and women argue about and then in groups draw up lists of the most common causes of arguments between men and women.

2 You are going to read an extract from a story in which a man and a woman who are living together go out for dinner. In the taxi and at the restaurant they 'fight'. What do you think they fight about?

3 The chapter the extract is taken from is called 'Wrinkled Linen' and includes the following sentences:

a) 'I don't want to eat there.'

b) 'No, I wasn't thinking about that. I was thinking about dinner and what to order.'

c) 'How can I live with someone who never talks to me?'

d) 'Now don't drink too much just because we're having a fight and you think you ought to drown your sorrows.'

e) 'What do the eighties mean to you, Mr Snuggles?'

4 Read the extract from *A Visit from the Footbinder* (Conflict 2) and, as you read, try to work out why the two characters are attracted to each other and why they frequently 'fight'?

5 In groups, list the main information you can gain from the extract about:
a) the woman;
b) the man;
c) the relationship between the two people.

6 Imagine you are a close friend of the couple in the extract and write a letter to the man and a letter to the woman telling each of them of your worries about their relationship and giving advice on how to improve it.

7 In pairs write the beginning of a short story in which a man and a woman are arguing in one of the following places:
a) a hotel;
b) a restaurant;
c) a station;
d) an airport;
e) a cinema.

8 Act out the extract you have written to another pair and then watch them acting out their story.

Then discuss the man/woman relationships in each of the stories.

3 Twinkle, Twinkle, Little Spy

1 You are going to read an extract from Chapter Fifteen of a spy novel. The chapter begins:

> Mann gave Mrs Bekuv no time to say goodbye to her husband: that was all part of his scheme. We sat in Mann's little office – originally intended for the duty nurse – and heard Andrei Bekuv walk down the corridor, calling his wife's name.
>
> Mann sat hunched over a desk in the corner, watching the dark storm-clouds come racing in from the Atlantic. The rain beat upon the windows and the morning was so dark that Mann needed the desk light in order to read. He looked at me and winked as Andrei Bekuv came back.
>
> 'Here we go,' said Mann softly.

In groups, decide:
a) who Mann is;

b) who Bekuv is;
c) what Mann's scheme is.

2 Read the extract from *Twinkle, Twinkle, Little Spy* (Conflict 3) and as you read, work out how accurate your predictions were in 1 above.

3 In groups, revise your answers to a)–c) in 1 above.

4 In groups, answer the following questions:
a) Why has Mann separated Mr and Mrs Bekuv?
b) Why do you think the KGB might want to kill Bekuv?
c) What is Mann ultimately trying to achieve?
d) What tricks does he use to try to achieve his goals?

5 In groups, write the letter to Bekuv's wife.

6 In groups, discuss the following statements:
a) Anything is justified in defence of the country's interests.
b) Spies play an important role in keeping world peace.
c) A country is not worth defending if it has to use immoral means to defend itself.
d) The worst criminal of all is the spy who betrays his own country.
e) It is justifiable to spy against your country if you believe that the policies and actions of your country are immoral.

7 In groups, map out an outline of a ten-chapter spy novel which has a woman spy as its main character.

4 One Flew Over the Cuckoo's Nest

1 Read the following short extract from a novel, and as you read, try to answer the following questions:
a) Who is the narrator?
b) Where does the incident take place?
c) Who are the black boys?
d) What point do you think the incident is used to illustrate?

> One Christmas at midnight on the button, at the old place, the ward door blows open with a crash, in comes a fat man with a beard, eyes ringed red by the cold and his nose just the colour of a cherry. The black boys get him cornered in the hall with flashlights. I see he's all tangled in the tinsel Public Relation has been stringing all over the

place, and he's stumbling around in it in the dark. He's shading his red eyes from the flashlights and sucking on his mustache.

'Ho ho ho,' he says. 'I'd like to stay but I must be hurrying along. Very tight schedule, ya know. Ho ho. Must be going . . .'

The black boys move in with the flashlights. They kept him with us six years before they discharged him, clean-shaven and skinny as a pole.

2 You are going to read a longer extract from the same novel. But first, form groups and:

a) Discuss your answers to the question in 1 above.

b) Predict the contents of the next page of the novel, a page which includes 'the Big Nurse', an adjustable wall clock, the Acutes, a fog in the ward and a game of cards.

3 Read the extract from *One Flew Over the Cuckoo's Nest* (Conflict 4) and as you read, try to visualize the scene.

4 Imagine that you are one of the patients on the ward and write a short article for a magazine entitled, 'A Day in My Life'.

When you have finished your article, show it to another learner. Ask for corrections and for suggestions for improvement. Then revise your article and give it in to the teacher who will decide which ones to 'publish' on the wall.

5 In pairs, write a version of the same scene, but narrated by the Big Nurse.

6 In groups, either:

a) work out and act a dramatic version of the scene from the novel;

or

b) work out and act, interviews between a television journalist and:
the narrator
the Big Nurse
one of the Acutes.

5 On the Yankee Station

1 You are going to read an extract from a short story which is set on board an American aircraft carrier during the Vietnam War.

In groups:

a) Note down anything that you know about the Vietnam War.

b) Discuss your attitudes to the Vietnam War.

2 In groups, discuss your reactions to the following statements:
   a) War is never justified and always evil.
   b) War always brutalizes the people who take part in it.
   c) Most wars are caused and run by people who do not actually have to fight in them.
   d) If the bomber pilot could see close-ups of the death and destruction he is causing he would not drop his bombs.
   e) If there were more women in charge of governments and armies there would be far fewer wars.

3 Read the extract from *On the Yankee Station* (Conflict 5) and as you read, try to work out the relationship and feelings between Lydecker and Pfitz.

4 In groups, answer the following questions:
   a) What did Lydecker like about the Crusader?
   b) What did Pfitz dislike about the Crusader?
   c) Why was Pfitz flying Crusaders and not Phantoms or Skyhawks?
   d) What did Lydecker and Pfitz enjoy about their different jobs?
   e) What was the relationship between Lydecker and Pfitz?
   f) How was Lydecker different from the other pilots?

5 In groups, either:
   a) Work out what you think happened when 'a seabird was sucked into the intake' and decide what effect it had on the relationship between Lydecker and Pfitz.

   As a group, practice taking it in turns to tell parts of your story.

   or

   b) Paint a picture (or series of pictures) conveying your interpretation of the bombing raids from the 'Yankee station'.

   or

   c) Write a poem called, 'Bomber Over Vietnam'.

   When you are ready, tell your story, display and explain your picture or read your poem to the class.

Dilemmas

1 A Dream of Africa

1 Think of the day when you first left home, and try to remember how you felt and what you did.

2 In groups, discuss your reactions to the following statements made by people about the day when they left home for the first time, and relate the statements to your own experience.
   a) 'I felt grown up, excited and above all, free.'
   b) 'I was terrified, but pretended to be brave.'
   c) 'I knew I would never see my father again.'
   d) 'I began to miss my family right away.'
   e) 'It was no big deal.'
   f) 'I immediately began to wish I'd listened to their advice.'
   g) 'I was out, away, soaring free.'

3 You are going to read an extract from a novel in which a nineteen-year-old youth goes to study overseas, despite the pleas of his mother.

   Before you read the extract, tell each other about books, songs, films and plays that you know which focus on the theme of leaving home.

4 Read the extract from *A Dream of Africa* (Dilemmas 1) and as you read, decide whether you think Fatoman was right to do what he did and to feel how he felt.

5 In groups, discuss the following statements:
   a) 'Fatoman was selfish to ignore his mother's wish for him to stay at home.'
   b) 'Fatoman's mother was selfish to try to prevent her son from going to France.'
   c) 'Fatoman was foolish to go to France without first of all finding out more about it.'

6 In groups, decide which of the following statements are true and which are false. Rewrite the false statements so that they become true.
   a) Fatoman's family lived in Conakry.

b) The man who advised the narrator was a fellow African.
c) Diabaté had been to Paris many times before.
d) The chapter is called 'A sleepless night' because Fatoman stayed awake all night worrying about his mother.
e) The uncles that Fatoman remembered were the people who were supposed to meet him in Paris.

7 Imagine that a young person is leaving home in your country (or another country that you know well) and think of how you would shoot the scene as the beginning of a film.

8 In groups, tell each other about your film scene and then choose one of the films described and practise acting it out.

9 Perform your scene for another group or for the class.

2 The British Museum is Falling Down

1 In groups, tell each other about any nightmares you can remember and discuss what you think caused you to have your nightmares.

2 Read the extract from *The British Museum is Falling Down* (Dilemmas 2) to yourself, and as you read decide whether you think it is a description of a real experience or of a dream.

3 In groups, decide whether you think the description is of a dream or a real event.

4 Discuss your decision with another group and give reasons for your decision.

5 In groups of four, practise acting out the scene.

6 Act your scene in front of another group, and discuss with them your interpretation of the scene.

7 Write one of the following:
a) a detailed explanation of the scene as a nightmare;
b) the next page of the novel;
c) an analysis of the author's reasons for including this scene in the novel;
d) a scene from a play satirizing bureaucracy.

Set your scene in either a post office, a police station, a railway information office or a government office.

3 A Man For All Seasons

1 In groups, draw up a list of any issues, beliefs or faiths that you would be prepared to suffer for.

Draw up a group list which all members agree on, and additional lists which reflect minority views of members of the group.

When you have drawn up your list, say which of the beliefs, etc. you would be prepared to:
a) lose a job for;
b) lose a lot of money for;
c) involve your family in a lot of suffering for;
d) go to prison for;
e) die for.

2 In groups, think of real and fictional characters who made great sacrifices for their beliefs. Tell each other about them and decide whether you think they were right to make the sacrifices they did.

Choose one of the characters you have been discussing, who you really admire. Tell another group (or the whole class) about this person and say why you admire him or her so much.

3 You are going to read an extract from a play in which the main character is visited in prison by his family. He knows that he is going to be executed for his beliefs and that his family are suffering, and are going to suffer even more. He could save himself and stop his family's suffering by telling a lie.

Read the extract (Dilemmas 3) and, as you read, decide whether More is right to sacrifice so much for a belief.

4 In groups, discuss the following questions:
a) Was More right to sacrifice so much for a belief?
b) What did Alice really think about her husband?
c) What did Alice really want her husband to do?
d) Why did More cry out 'Oh, Sweet Jesus! These plain, simple men!'?

5 In groups of six, practise acting out the scene, with five people taking parts and the sixth person acting as director, advising the actors.

When you are ready, act out the scene to another group. Then watch their version of the scene, and when they have finished, discuss with them the similarities and differences in your interpretations of the scenes.

6 In groups, answer the following questions:
a) What is Margaret trying to do to her father?
b) Why does More tell Margaret, 'The King's more merciful than you.'?
c) Why does More compliment his wife on her custard and her dress?
d) Why does Alice react so harshly to More's compliments?
e) What does More mean by 'a "good" death'?
f) Why does Alice respond by saying, 'Your death's no good to me.'?
g) Why is the jailer so insistent that the family leave More exactly at seven?
h) Why do you think More's family were allowed to visit him?
i) Why do you think they will not be allowed to visit him again?

7 The extract you have read does not tell you why More is in prison or what belief he sacrificed so much for.

Find out as much as you can about Sir Thomas More and his death (e.g. from encyclopaedias, from history books, from reading *A Man For All Seasons,* etc.) and then write an essay, poem or extract from a biography entitled 'Why Sir Thomas More Died'. You can write it as yourself, as Alice or Margaret More or as the Jailer.

4 Forty Years On

1 You are going to read an extract from a play which involves a trial. The play is both farcical and satirical and is in the style of the Theatre of the Absurd. The trial involves Neville Chamberlain being accused of a ridiculous crime.

Before you read the extract, divide into groups and try to find answers to the following questions:
a) Who was Neville Chamberlain?
b) What did he do in September 1938?
c) Who lives at 10 Downing Street?
d) What did Chamberlain look like?
e) What was the reaction in Britain to Chamberlain in September 1938?
f) What is the current view of Chamberlain and his actions of 1938?
g) What is meant by Appeasement?
h) What is the normal procedure in a British court of law?
i) What is the Theatre of the Absurd?

2 Half the groups in the class become A groups and half become B groups.

The A groups should read extract A from *Forty Years On* (Dilemmas 4) and the B groups should read extract B.

3 When you have read your extract, discuss it with the other members of your group.

Explain difficult bits to each other. Look up words you do not understand and try to locate and explain the jokes.

4 Practise acting your extract with the purpose of making it as funny as possible.

5 Each A group should act their extract to a B group and should try to make them laugh. The B group should then act their extract to the A group and try to make them laugh.

The groups should then discuss what they did and did not find funny in the two extracts.

6 Each group should read the extract they have not yet read and then answer the following questions:
a) What is Chamberlain really charged with?
b) What is the significance of Chamberlain replying, 'I'm not sure.'?
c) What is the significance of the judge saying, 'I know the trial procedure backwards.'?
d) What is the point being made through the references to 'moustaches'?
e) Why does Chamberlain mention that Hitler was 'very fond of dogs'?
f) What is the significance of Czechoslovakia pointing at the audience?
g) What is the point of the counsel mentioning that Chamberlain was born in Birmingham?
h) What points do you think that the writer is making in this extract from his play?

7 In groups, select a famous figure from history and then work out a comic scene in which that character is put on trial in a British court.

Act out your scene for the class and try to make them laugh.

When devising your scene, try to include slapstick, puns, absurdisms and satire and try to attack targets that will be recognized by the audience.

Bibliography

The following is a list of the books from which extracts have been taken for *Openings*. It is arranged in alphabetical order by title, for each category of book, and section references are given for the extracts from the books. Both hardback and paperback editions are cited wherever possible.

1 Non-fiction

Journey to Wembley, Brian James, Sport 2 (Marshall Cavendish 1977)
The Greatest – My Own Story, Muhammad Ali with Richard Durham, Sport 1 (Mayflower Books 1976)
Unreliable Memoirs, Clive James, Growing Up 3 and Education 3 (first published 1980 by Jonathan Cape, then Pan 1981)

2 Novels

A Dream of Africa, Camara Laye, Dilemmas 1 (first published 1966 by French, then Fontana 1979)
Billy Liar, Keith Waterhouse, Family 3 (first published 1959 by Michael Joseph, then Penguin 1962, reprinted 1977)
Close Encounters of the Third Kind, Steven Spielberg, Society 4 (first UK edition 1978 by Sphere)
Efuru, Flora Nwapa, Love 1 (Heinemann Educational 1966)
How Far Can You Go?, David Lodge, Love 2 (first published 1980 by Martin Secker and Warburg, then Penguin 1981)
Indecent Exposure, Tom Sharpe, Society 7 (first published 1973 by Martin Secker and Warburg, then Pan 1974)
Looks and Smiles, Barry Hines, Sport 3 (first published 1981 by Michael Joseph, then Penguin 1983)
Midnight's Children, Salman Rushdie, Society 5 (first published 1981 by Jonathan Cape, then Pan 1982)

No Longer at Ease, Chinua Achebe, Growing Up 2 (first published 1960 by William Heinemann, then in the Heinemann African Writers Series 1963, reprinted 1981)

One Flew Over the Cuckoo's Nest, Ken Kesey, Confict 4 (first published 1962 by Methuen, then Pan 1973)

The British Museum is Falling Down, David Lodge, Dilemmas 2 (first published 1965 by MacGibbon and Kee, then Penguin 1981)

The Chip-Chip Gatherers, Shiva Naipaul, Education 2 (first published 1973 by Andre Deutsch, then Penguin 1976)

The Ginger Man, J. P. Donleavy, Family 6 (first UK edition Corgi 1963, then Penguin 1968, reprinted 1978)

The Graduate, Charles Webb, Growing Up 1 (first published 1964 by Constable, then Penguin 1968)

The Heart of the Matter, Graham Greene, Love 3 (first published 1948 by William Heinemann, then Penguin 1962, reprinted 1969)

The Human Factor, Graham Greene, Family 4 (first published 1978 by Bodley Head, then Penguin 1978)

The Interpreters, Wole Soyinka, Society 3 (first published 1965 by Andre Deutsch, then Fontana 1972)

The Malayan Trilogy, Anthony Burgess, Education 5 (first published 1956 by William Heinemann, then Penguin 1972, reprinted 1981)

The Natural Order, Ursula Bentley, Education 4 (first published 1982 by Martin Secker and Warburg, then Arrow 1983)

The Public Image, Muriel Spark, Society 6 (Macmillan 1968)

The Rain Forest, Olivia Manning, Family 1 (first published 1974 by William Heinemann, then Penguin 1977)

The Right True End, Stan Barstow, Family 2 (first published 1976 by Michael Joseph, then Corgi 1978)

The World According to Garp, John Irving, Growing Up 4 and Society 8 (first published 1978 by Victor Gollancz, then Corgi 1979)

Twinkle, Twinkle, Little Spy, Len Deighton, Conflict 3 (first published 1976 by Jonathan Cape, then Triad/Panther 1977)

3 Plays

A Man For All Seasons, Robert Bolt, Dilemmas 3 (first published 1960 by William Heinemann, then Penguin 1963: New English Dramatists 6)

Forty Years On, Alan Bennett, Dilemmas 4 (first published 1969 by Faber and Faber)

Professional Foul, Tom Stoppard, Sport 4, from Stoppard: *Every Good Boy Deserves Favour and Professional Foul* (first published 1978 by Faber and Faber)

The Birthday Party, Harold Pinter, Conflict 1 (Eyre Methuen 1976)

The Happy Haven, John Arden, Society 1 (Penguin 1962: New English Dramatists 4)

The Norman Conquests, Alan Ayckbourn, Family 5 (first published 1975 by Chatto and Windus, then Penguin 1977)

4 Poems

'My Name Blew Like a Horn Among the Payira', Love 5, from 'Song of Lawino' by Okot P'Bitek, from *African Voices*, selected by Howard Sergeant (Evans Brothers 1973)

'Schoolmaster', Yevtushenko, Education 1, from *Selected Poems by Yevtushenko* (Penguin 1962, reprinted 1973)

'Telephone Conversation', Wole Soyinka, Society 9, from *Modern Poetry from Africa*, edited by Gerald Moore and Ulli Beier (Penguin 1963)

5 Short stories

'A Visit from the Footbinder', Conflict 2, from a collection with that title by Emily Prager (Chatto and Windus 1983)

'On the Yankee Station', Conflict 5, from a collection with that title by William Boyd (first published 1981 by Hamish Hamilton, then Penguin 1982)

'Sentence of Death', Love 4, from *Merseymart's Scouse Stories* by Terry Morgan (Merseymart 1982)

'The Rabbits Who Caused All the Trouble', Society 2, from *The Thurber Carnival* by James Thurber (first published 1945 by Penguin, then this abridged edition Penguin 1953)

List of Authors

The following is an alphabetical list of the authors whose work has been included in this book. After each name is a reference to the work(s) from which an extract has been taken and a section reference for the extract(s). This is followed by a brief description of the author plus suggestions for further reading.

Chinua Achebe

No Longer at Ease (Growing Up 2)

Chinua Achebe is a Nigerian who is considered by many to be the greatest African novelist.

Suggestions for further reading:
A Man Of The People
Things Fall Apart

Muhammad Ali

The Greatest – My Own Story (Sport 1)

Muhammad Ali first won the World Heavyweight Boxing title in 1964. From then on he dominated his sport and became a world famous celebrity. He now travels the world doing charity work.

John Arden

The Happy Haven (Society 1)

John Arden is a leading British dramatist.

Suggestion for further reading:
Sergeant Musgrave's Dance

Alan Ayckbourn

The Norman Conquests (Family 5)

Alan Ayckbourn is an Englishman who is one of the most prolific and successful of contemporary dramatists.

Suggestions for further reading:
Absurd Person Singular
Bedroom Farce
Taking Steps

Stan Barstow

The Right True End (Family 2)

Stan Barstow is an Englishman who has made his reputation by writing novels from, and about, the north of England.

Suggestions for further reading:
A Kind of Loving
A Raging Calm
The Watchers on the Shore

Ursula Bentley

The Natural Order (Education 4)

Ursula Bentley is English but has travelled widely in Europe and the United States. She was selected by the Book Marketing Council as one of the 20 best young writers for 1983.

Alan Bennett

Forty Years On (Dilemmas 4)

Alan Bennett is an English dramatist who is renowned for his satirical plays.

Okot P'Bitek

'My Name Blew Like a Horn Among the Payira' from 'Song of Lawino' (Love 5)

Okot P'Bitek is a Ugandan who is famous for his two narrative poems 'Song of Lawino' and 'Song of Ocol'.

Robert Bolt

A Man For All Seasons (Dilemmas 3)

Robert Bolt is a dramatist who made his name with *A Man For All Seasons*, but is also held in high regard for his many film scripts.

William Boyd

'On the Yankee Station' (Conflict 5)

William Boyd was born in Ghana and grew up there and in Nigeria. He was a lecturer in English Literature at St Hilda's College, Oxford, but he has been a full-time writer since 1983.

Suggestions for further reading:
A Good Man In Africa
An Ice Cream War

Anthony Burgess

The Malayan Trilogy (Education 5)

Anthony Burgess is one of the most famous and successful of English contemporary novelists.

Suggestions for further reading:
Earthly Powers
The Clockwork Orange

Len Deighton

Twinkle, Twinkle, Little Spy (Conflict 3)

Len Deighton is a Londoner who is renowned as one of the best contemporary writers of spy stories.

Suggestions for further reading:
Funeral in Berlin
Spy Story
Game, Set and Match (a trilogy)

J. P. Donleavy

The Ginger Man (Family 6)

J. P. Donleavy is an American who is famous for his outrageously funny novels and plays.

Suggestions for further reading:
A Singular Man
The Beastly Beatitudes of Balthazar B.
The Destinies of Davy Dancer, Gentlemen.

Graham Greene

The Heart of the Matter (Love 3)
The Human Factor (Family 4)

Graham Greene is an Englishman who is one of the greatest of living novelists. He has written many outstanding novels, entertainments, stories and film scripts.

Suggestions for further reading:
Burnt Out Case
Brighton Rock
Our Man in Havana
The Comedians
The Third Man
The Quiet American
Travels with My Aunt

Barry Hines

Looks and Smiles (Sport 3)

Barry Hines was born in Yorkshire, England. He became a PE teacher and then a full-time novelist and playwright.

Suggestions for further reading:
The Blinder
Kes

John Irving

The World According to Garp (Growing Up 4 and Society 8)

John Irving is an American who specializes in black comedies and who achieved international recognition with *The World According to Garp.*

Suggestions for further reading:
The Hotel New Hampshire
The Water Method Man

Brian James

Journey to Wembley (Sport 2)

Brian James is a British sport journalist who wrote *Journey to Wembley* about his experiences following the FA Cup from the qualifying rounds to the Final.

Clive James

Unreliable Memoirs (Growing Up 3 and Education 3)

Clive James is an Australian who now lives in Cambridge in England. He became famous as the television critic for the *Observer* and as a television personality.

Suggestion for further reading:
Brilliant Creatures

Ken Kesey

One Flew Over the Cuckoo's Nest (Conflict 4)

Ken Kesey is an American. His novel, *One Flew Over the Cuckoo's Nest,* has become a modern classic and has been made into a major film starring Jack Nicholson.

Suggestion for further reading:
Sometimes a Great Notion

Camara Laye

A Dream of Africa (Dilemmas 1)

Camara Laye was born in Guinea in 1924. He was educated in Conakry and France and became the first African author to achieve international acclaim when his first book, *The African Child,* was published.

Suggestion for further reading:
The African Child

David Lodge

How Far Can You Go? (Love 2)
The British Museum Is Falling Down (Dilemmas 2)

David Lodge is Professor of Modern English Literature at the University of Birmingham in England. He is considered to be one of the leading contemporary British novelists.

Suggestions for Further Reading
Changing Places
Small World

Olivia Manning

The Rain Forest (Family 1)

Olivia Manning was born in England, spent much of her youth in Ireland and then lived in Bucharest, Egypt and Jerusalem before settling in London in 1946. There she wrote novels, short stories and film scripts. She was awarded the OBE in 1976 and died in 1980.

Suggestions for further reading:
The Balkan Trilogy
The Levant Trilogy

Terry Morgan

'Sentence of Death' from *Scouse Stories* (Love 4)

Terry Morgan is a Liverpool journalist who writes humorous stories for a Liverpool newspaper called *Merseymart.*

Shiva Naipaul

The Chip-Chip Gatherers (Education 2)

Shiva Naipaul was born in Trinidad in 1945. He is the brother of the prolific Trinidadian novelist V. S. Naipaul.

Suggestion for further reading:
Fireflies

Flora Nwapa

Efuru (Love 1)

Flora Nwapa is a Nigerian who has worked as a teacher, an Education Officer, an Assistant Registrar and as Commissioner for Lands, Survey and Urban Development in East Central State. She was the first Nigerian woman to be published.

Suggestions for further reading:
Idu
This is Lagos

Harold Pinter

The Birthday Party (Conflict 1)

Harold Pinter is a Londoner who is famous for his plays and screenplays. He has been described as 'our best living playwright' (*The Times*).

Suggestions for further reading:
The Caretaker
The Homecoming
No Man's Land

Emily Prager

'A Visit from the Footbinder' (Conflict 2)

Emily Prager is an American, who lives in New York. She is a journalist and a television personality. *A Visit from the Footbinder* is her first collection of stories.

Salman Rushdie

Midnight's Children (Society 5)

Salman Rushdie was born in Bombay in 1947, and now lives in London. He won the Booker Prize in 1981 for *Midnight's Children.*

Suggestion for further reading:
Shame

Tom Sharpe

Indecent Exposure (Society 7)

Tom Sharpe is an Englishman who was deported from South Africa, became a lecturer in History at the Cambridge College of Arts and Technology and then became famous for his outrageous, satirical novels.

Suggestions for further reading:
Blott on the Landscape
Porterhouse Blue
Riotous Assembly
The Wilt Alternative
Wilt

Wole Soyinka

'Telephone Conversation' (Society 9)
The Interpreters (Society 3)

Wole Soyinka is a Nigerian who has achieved international acclaim for his plays, his poems and his first novel, *The Interpreters.*

Suggestions for further reading:
Ake
Lion and The Jewel

Muriel Spark

The Public Image (Society 6)

Muriel Spark is an English woman who has produced a number of highly regarded novels.

Suggestions for further reading:
The Ballad of Peckham Rye
The Girls of Slender Means
The Prime of Miss Jean Brodie

Steven Spielberg

Close Encounters of The Third Kind (Society 4)

Steven Spielberg is an American who has achieved fame as a film director.

Tom Stoppard

Professional Foul (Sport 4)

Tom Stoppard is an Englishman who has produced some of the best plays of the last decade.

Suggestions for further reading:
Enter a Free Man *Night and Day*
Jumpers *Travesties*

James Thurber

'The Rabbits Who Caused All the Trouble' from *The Thurber Carnival* (Society 2)

James Thurber is an American satirist who is especially famous for his cartoons and his humorous anecdotes and short stories.

Suggestion for further reading:
The Best in Me

Keith Waterhouse

Billy Liar (Family 3)

Keith Waterhouse is an Englishman who specializes in comic plays, novels, television series and journalism.

Suggestions for further reading:
Billy Liar on the Moon *The Bucket Shop*
Jubb

Charles Webb

The Graduate (Growing Up 1)

Charles Webb is an American whose first novel, *The Graduate,* was made into a very successful film starring Dustin Hoffman.

Yevtushenko

'Schoolmaster' (Education 1)

Yevtushenko is a Russian who is considered by many to be one of the greatest of contemporary poets.

Suggestion for further reading:
Yevtushenko – Selected Poems